THE ALCHEMY OF T`___
A Jungian Perspective.

Cover Image: *An Alchemist*. Oil on canvas. By Edward Charles Barnes
Credit: Wellcome Collection https://wellcomecollection.org/works/bd9fjaz7
Attribution: 4.0 International (CC BY 4.0) https://creativecommons.org/licenses/by/4.0

THE ALCHEMY OF TYRANNY

A JUNGIAN PERSPECTIVE

William K. Grevatt

The work is difficult and strewn with obstacles; the alchemical opus is dangerous. Right at the beginning you meet the dragon, the chthonic spirit, the devil, or as the alchemists called it, the blackness or nigredo, and this encounter produces suffering. 'Matter' suffers right up to the final disappearance of the blackness; in psychological terms, the soul finds itself in the throes of melancholy, locked up in a struggle with the 'shadow.' The mystery of the coniunctio, the central mystery of alchemy, aims precisely at the synthesis of opposites, the assimilation of the blackness, the integration of the devil.

— C.G. JUNG, RESPONDING IN AN INTERVIEW WITH MIRCEA ELIADE (1952, P. 228)

CONTENTS

CHAPTER ONE

From Prague to Budapest: A
Journey through Central Europe

*Democracy may, after all, turn out to be an historical accident, a
brief parenthesis that is closing before our eyes.*

— JEAN FRANCOIS REVEL, HOW DEMOCRACIES PERISH (1983)

W e expected to enjoy a leisurely twelve days in central
Europe, cruising down the Danube and stepping off
the boat to explore medieval towns and villages,
going on hikes and bike rides though the gorgeous countryside—a
respite from the analytic practice, as well as teaching and admin-
istrative duties running a non-profit Jungian training institute.
What transpired revealed itself to be quite another journey al-
together—something that would leave indelible marks upon us.

We began our sojourn in Prague with a visit to The Speculum
Alchemiae, a jewel of the medieval alchemical world that was
only rediscovered in 2002, when massive flooding on the Vltava
River created a huge sinkhole in the street in front of the house at
1 Hastalska. This revealed a series of underground alchemical
laboratories dating back to the 16th century, attributed to the
Habsburg ruler of that period, Emperor Rudolph II.

Astrology and alchemy were regarded as mainstream scientific
fields in Renaissance Prague, though not approved by the Roman
Catholic Church. Rudolph was apparently deeply interested in
both these new sciences, and his lifelong quest was to find the
Philosopher's Stone. This was his own private and secret alchem-

ical laboratory that was hidden underground in the Jewish quarter of the city, away from prying canonical Church eyes. It is worth noting that Rudolf is also the ruler in many of the legends of the Golem of Prague, [1] adding to his mystical reputation. The house itself at the current location of the museum dates back to 900 ce, which means that this house is probably the second oldest building in Prague.

The house in Haštalská Street is located on what was then the most important medieval European trade route, the "Grand Via," which was thousands of miles long and ran from the north of Spain across the whole of Europe to the Far East. The central location of Prague, between East and West, made a natural trading point.

From the back of the main floor we locate an ancient hidden stairwell and begin descending down uneven stone steps in a circular formation, until we reach the first of four underground caverns, seemingly carved out of the natural rock. As you turn right at the bottom of the stairwell, you are seized by the sight of the first chamber, about twenty feet square, filled with a large spiral-shaped stone fireplace and upon it fantastical looking-glass containers with long sloping mouths of every size and shape. You cannot escape the feeling of being transported back in time 500 years to this authentic medieval alchemical laboratory.

[1] The most famous golem narrative involves Judah Loew ben Bezalel, the late 16th-century rabbi of Prague, also known as the Maharal, who reportedly "created a golem out of clay from the banks of the Vltava River and brought it to life through rituals and Hebrew incantations to defend the Prague ghetto from anti-Semitic attacks" and pogroms (myjewish-learning.com).

This room served the distillation process; a second chamber served as the storage space for the various herbs used for the process; a third chamber was devoted to the manufacture of the glass vials and larger containers. Underground tunnels were discovered that connected to the three most important places in the city: Prague Castle, the Old Town Hall, and the military barracks.

Rumor has it that the pope, discovering word of Rudolph's alchemical interests, sent a Vatican emissary to confront Rudolph with his illegal activities, which the church hierarchy expressly forbade. But Rudolph needed not have worried, for the emissary himself, it turns out, was also a practicing alchemist.

Jung felt that when he discovered alchemy, he had stumbled upon a historical counterpart of his psychology of the unconscious. The principle similarity was that of projection. The alchemist, while attempting to create gold from the four base elements of mercury, lead, sulphur, and salt, was "seeing" certain properties in that matter. But, in fact, what the alchemist was seeing and experiencing were projections from his own unconscious. What he was experiencing had nothing to do with the matter itself. (This concept of projection is a theme to which I will return.) In a 1952 interview with Mircea Eliade, for the Paris based Combat Magazine, Jung stated:

> *The alchemical operations are real, only this reality was not physical but psychological. Alchemy represents the projection of a drama both cosmic and spiritual in laboratory terms. The opus magnum had two aims; the rescue of the human soul and the salvation of the cosmos. What the alchemists called 'matter' was in reality the [unconscious] self. The 'soul of the world,' the anima mundi, which was identified with the spiritus mercurious, was imprisoned in matter. It is for this reason that the alchemists believed in the 'truth of the matter.' (p.228)*

Fast forward to 2018 when we were about to discover just what was currently brewing in the alchemical cauldron of Central Europe, beginning in the Czech Republic, followed by stops in Austria and then Hungary. Leaving Prague and its rich alchemical history, we travelled fifty miles south to another medieval city, Cesky Krumluv, where time again seems to have stood still. Krumluv literally means "twisted," which the Vlatava River does here numerous times, creating a natural moat around a small isthmus that contains an entire medieval village crowned by a 13th-century castle.

Within this somewhat spectacular setting, we were shocked to hear our guide inform us that 55% of the current Czech population would rather live under a Communistic system, despite almost three decades now living under a democracy. Democracy took hold after the Velvet Revolution in 1989, which allowed the countries to peacefully break away from the yoke of Soviet Communist rule. Our guide further explained that under the Communist Soviet system, which ruled from 1948 to 1989, every adult was assigned both a job and an apartment. This may not seem much to those of us coming from an affluent North American lifestyle, but for a people who have had difficulty adjusting to a free-market system over the last thirty years, it is significant.

To understand the present situation in the Czech Republic, one has to explore its complicated history at least back to World War II. It was in 1938 when the Czechs were sold out by the West to appease Hitler (the Munich Agreement): half of all their land was ceded to the Nazis, without their consent—an act of appeasement that not only famously failed but emboldened Hitler to go to war.

After the war, Czech nationalists returned from both London and Moscow in large numbers, but democracy gave way to Communism and a more open attitude towards the Soviet Union, which had liberated the country from the Germans. At first elected democratically in 1946, the Communists took power in a coup in 1948, establishing a single party state.

It took until 1989 and the Velvet Revolution, led by the playwright Vaclav Havel, for democracy to be restored under a multiparty system that remains today. Havel brought the nation into both NATO and the European Union and the liberal values of the West. But today those values are under fire. James Kirchick (2017), in his book The End of Europe, writes:

> *Havel's death seemingly marked the passing not only of a great man but also a legacy. His vision of an open, pluralistic, and confident Europe has been neglected if not out-*

right repudiated, in his own country and elsewhere across the continent. Havel's immediate successor, Vaclav Klaus, a friend and ally of Vladimir Putin, forsook his own nation's history as a target of Warsaw Pact invasion and supported Russia unequivocally when it invaded and annexed Ukrainian territory. The current Czech president, Milos Zeman, whose campaign was largely funded by the Russian state oil firm Lukoil, is even more slavish in deference to Moscow. (pp. 224–225)

From a depth psychological perspective, what is happening in the unconscious of both the leaders and the electorate of the Czech Republic? Why is it that a majority of people would still rather live under a totalitarian regime than a free democracy? Consciously, at least to us in the West who have grown up with liberal democratic values, this seems obscene. But the conscious collective attitude of many in the Czech Republic (most notably outside of liberal Prague) is that they do not trust the liberal democratic values of the West, and would prefer the seeming security of living in a totalitarian state, run by a strong man. Given Europe's violent past in the last century with its two horrific world wars, this seems a very chilling and puzzling conclusion. What are they "seeing into" this matter that we do not see?

Evidence of this violent past is palpable at our next stop at the Mauthausen Concentration Camp, just over the border in Austria. From 1938 to 1945 Mauthausen, along with its satellite camps, housed over 350,000 Jewish and political prisoners from many different countries, including Poland, Czechoslovakia, Russia, Hungary, Yugoslavia, France, Spain, and the Netherlands. Of these only about 90,000 survived. The stated goal of the camp was "to work you to death."

This working of prisoners to death was accomplished through the dangerous operation of a large granite quarry without any safety standards or proper equipment. Here hundreds of SS guards cruelly tortured their prisoners at every opportunity. Each evening, at the end of the workday, each prisoner was forced to carry a granite stone weighing over 100 pounds up 186 steps (named the "stairs of death") to the top of the camp—not because this was efficient, but only because the guards wanted to make them suffer.

The prisoners were made to construct the entire camp, while being half-starved to death. The twenty-foot granite walls extended for about a mile in circumference, encircling many acres of land and buildings that included the barracks, offices, hospital, gas chambers, and crematorium. On these grounds the sense of horror is overwhelming, and remains with me now. What were the Nazis projecting onto the Jews, homosexuals, gypsies, the disabled, and intelligentsia that they brutally and systematically killed them by the tens of thousands?

Our Austrian guide Therese carefully explained to us that every inhabitant of the town of Mauthausen (largely Austrian Catholics) was complicit with what went on at the camp, as the thousands of SS officers who worked at the camp were housed with the town's families. Throughout the war, boxcars unloaded thousands of new prisoners at the train depot; where they disembarked and were forced to march three miles through town and uphill to the camp.

Mauthausen was the last concentration camp liberated at the end of World War II, in May 1945, by American troops. Outside the main entrance to the camp several monuments from various countries commemorate the death and torture of its citizens who were imprisoned there. One stood out to me, carved out on it the simple words "Be Alert".

I had the feeling talking with Austrians that the fascist past is never too far from the surface. Evidence of this is that a right-wing anti-immigration party (the Freedom Party) has recently come to power in a coalition with the Austrian Peoples Party. Many of their members are now assigned to important cabinet posts, including immigration. The Freedom Party was founded in 1956 by former SS officers. Author and essayist James Kirchick (2017) articulates a valid point:

Rising support across Europe for xenophobic, populist par-
ties is partly the result of a constricted political discourse
in which decent ordinary people are told that not only
plainly visible social phenomena don't exist (i.e. a genuine
terrorist threat is created when admitting tens of thou-
sands of people into your country from the Middle East) but
also that voicing concerns about these allegedly nonexistent
phenomena is racist.... by not allowing for any dissent or
open debate of these issues in liberal democracies such as
Sweden and Germany, "European elites have only fed the
monster they hope to destroy." (p. 121)

As one example, in 2015 Germany perhaps should not have admitted over one million refugees in that single year. But to protest against this at the time was viewed in Germany as being racist and xenophobic, which of course is not necessarily the case. While Angela Merkel's government demonstrated a huge humanitarian warmth towards the one million displaced citizens from Syria due to the brutal civil war there, many Germans found it too overwhelming a prospect to have to assimilate them within German society. This highly consequential step may have not been considered from a sufficiently comprehensive perspective.

The last stop on our journey was Budapest. It is spectacularly framed by the hills of Buda on the west, the bustling metropolis of Pest to the east, and the wide, fast flowing Danube River in between. The physical beauty of Budapest is stunning. The politics, unfortunately, are rather ugly. The Victor Orban–led Fidesz Party government, since winning a landslide election in 2010, which it further solidified in 2014 and 2018 after gerrymandering the electoral districts, has, according to Kirchick, (2017, pp. 56–57):

...re-written the constitution, centralized power in the
executive, weakened checks and balances, empowered an

oligarchic class, dispensed state awards and ceded cultural policy to extreme right-wing figures, rendered parliament a rubber stamp, overhauled public media institutions into partisan outlets, harassed civil society, and reoriented Hungary's traditionally Atlanticist and pro-European foreign policy toward Russia and other authoritarian regimes.

Already enforcing the strictest "closed door" policy across the European Union for immigrants at its borders, the Fidesz government, while we were in Budapest, issued new legal measures "allowing for the prosecution and jailing of human rights workers and volunteers for providing services, advice or support to migrants and asylum seekers" (Laura King, Los Angeles Times, June 29, 2018, pages A-1 and A-4).

The new Hungarian system of government is being called an "illiberal democracy," but it more closely resembles a totalitarian state. Orban is consciously dismantling the democracy in a steady, systematic fashion, replacing it with tyranny, and telling its people that this change will be good for them. Kirchick (2017, pp. 63–64) surmises:

Harnessing popular fears about the stream of migrants pouring into Europe, Orban has greatly expanded his profile across the continent...now internationally renowned as the last defender of "Christian" Europe against Muslim hordes. . . . By anointing himself flag-bearer of those demanding a Europe with barbed wire fences, Orban has neutralized scrutiny of his domestic policies and rendered his "illiberal state" model respectable.

Taking a step back to see beyond Hungary, Austria, and the Czech Republic in Central Europe, one is further struck by how these nationalist populist parties are gaining ground all across Europe. In the west this includes England with Nigel Farage of the

United Kingdom Independence Party (UKIP) and now Boris Johnson (Conservative leader and now Prime Minister) dealing with a messy Brexit; France with Marine Le Pen and her the National Front Party; the Sweden Democrats and the True Finns in the north; and Greece's Golden Dawn in the south. "In the programs and statements of these parties," observes Columbia's University's Robert Paxton, "one hears echoes of classical fascist themes: fears of decadence and decline; assertion of national and cultural identity; a threat by unassimilable foreigners to national identity and good social order; and the need for greater authority to deal with these problems (as cited in Albright, 2018, p. 182).

There is no doubt that liberal democratic governments in both the United States and Europe have not always dealt honestly with the real problems of immigration and those left behind within the modern global economy for at least thirty years now. This failure has created an opportunity for ultra-right-wing nationalist parties to gain an increasing foothold among their frustrated electorates. Many view their leaders as being tone deaf and self-serving, taking turns at the helm of the national government, not seeming to care about the voters but rather catering to elite special interests. In the 2016 U.S. election, Trump changed all that. A vote for Trump was a vote against the party establishments who many believed were not listening any more. We are still in shock three years later—and with good reason.

Psychologically speaking, Trump emerged through the dark shadow of this country's history, from the very bowels of the earth, like a Trickster archetype manifesting itself from the depths to warn humankind, and its governments, that all are now in peril if they cannot find a new ruling principle (Grevatt, 2018; Jung, 1954). Uncaring establishment parties, along with an extreme "politically correct" left liberalism, have constellated an equal and opposite force of extreme right-wing values, with each side demonizing the other while they lose their ability to think clearly from a balanced and objective position.

When you distill tyranny down to its base elements, you always find the same rancid ingredients: hate, fear, doubt, anger, racism, anti-Semitism, anti-immigration, and a demonization of anything "other"; a pure and utterly unconscious projection of the shadow onto that other. And when this projection is being consciously promoted by authoritarian rulers around the world, including the likes of Putin, Trump, and Orban, it is nothing less than incarnated evil.

Our problem, at its root, is not political but moral and spiritual in nature, where the concepts of "the greater good and "We, the people" have all but disappeared. Seventy-five years after World War II and the forward movement of democratic liberalism throughout the world, the ground is shifting again, and those hard-fought-for values are under increasing duress. Consistent with Jung's concept of psychological enantiodromia, the pendulum is swinging back now in the opposite direction, and we find ourselves to be in a collective global regression of these liberal democratic values. In 1994 Vaclav told the European Parliament:

> If the future European order does not emerge from a broadening European Union, based upon the best European values and willing to transmit and defend them, the organization of the future could well fall into the hands of a cast of fools, fanatics, populists and demagogues waiting for their chance and determined to promote the worst in Europe. (http://www.europarl.europa.eu)

This same issue now faces other former liberal democracies, including Australia, Brazil, France, Great Britain, Greece, Turkey, and the United States, to name a significant few. The question is, can the best inclinations of these countries defeat their worst inclinations, the embers of which are daily stoked by their demagogic leaders?

In the chapters that follow I will break down this dark shift to the extreme political right as it manifests globally, analyzing this phenomenon from an alchemical and depth psychological perspective. Along the way, I will explore the projections that are occurring both consciously and unconsciously within the leaders and the populations of nations where this dark shift to the right is occurring. I will discuss how we, as individuals, can become more conscious of the psychodynamic factors at work, and thereby strive to always be alert.

CHAPTER TWO

Confronting the Trickster:
The Mercurial Trump

Like many other myths, the trickster myth is supposed to have a therapeutic effect. It holds the earlier low intellectual and moral level before the eyes of the more highly developed individual, so that he shall not forget how things looked yesterday.

— C. G. JUNG (1954)

The shift to the radical right in the United States has been punctuated by the election of Donald Trump in 2016, who has pledged, with his dark populist nationalist fervor, to Make America Great Again—a thinly transparent message that he will make America great again for white Americans and miserable for everyone else.

Jung might say of the current situation that the trickster has got us. We were laughing at Trump, thinking it was a dark force that could not reach us. But we didn't understand that the dark force was within us as well. And now he's got us, and the most powerful nation in the world is in the hands of the trickster. And we have no idea what trick will be played on us next.

Jung explains that the archetype of the trickster represents a repressed aspect of the dark shadow that becomes "split off" from the personality, on both individual and collective levels, because we would rather not have to deal with it. Jung (1954) states:

The [trickster] figure works, because secretly it partici-
pates in the observer's psyche and appears as its reflection,
though it is not recognized as such. It is split off from
his consciousness and consequently behaves like an au-
tonomous personality. The trickster is a collective shadow
figure, a reflection of all the inferior traits of character in
individuals. (par. 484)

Donald Trump's personality resounds with the repressed inferior character traits of individuals in our society. He is narcissistic, reactive, and unreflective. During his campaign to become president and since then he has stirred up feelings of hatred, fear, racism, misogyny, and xenophobia. Now that he's elected, some of his supporters feel free to express these repressed feelings in damaging and divisive ways. This has been amply demonstrated in the neo-Nazi and Ku Klux Klan march that took place in Charlottesville, Virginia in August of 2017, which resulted in the death of three people; the assassination by an anti-Semitic gunman of eleven elderly members of a Jewish synagogue in Pittsburg in October 2018, and most recently in the racially motivated shooting and killing of 22 people (mostly Hispanic) in El Paso, Texas in August of 2019. There is undoubtedly a feeling of being "locked up" in an epic struggle with the dark energy he has brought into our daily lives.

Clearer still is his behavior as an "autonomous personality." We never know what direction Trump is going in because he doesn't know. Further, he reserves the right to change his mind at any time and to declare what he said on national television one hour ago as "fake news" if it suits his twisted mind. Such an attitude is what we could describe, in the kindest of terms, as being "mercurial"; it is the Roman god Mercury (synonymous with the Greek god Hermes) who is associated with the trickster archetype.

Hermes is the god responsible for carrying messages from

heaven to earth, from god to humankind, a divine messenger. Edward Edinger (1994) tells us that "he is a wind god and he moves with the wind. He is the god of revelation, the bringer of dreams, the guide of the dark way.... Hermes is the great trespasser, a crosser of boundaries.... He can be ambiguous, false and cunning, and that gets him into places that absolute light and clarity could never enter" (pp. 30–31)

The crosser of boundaries, the great trespasser, false and cunning . . . sounding familiar? But here's the catch: Trump is not living out the trickster archetype; the trickster archetype is living him out. As Jung famously put it, it is not so much that we have a complex, but rather that the complex has us. (We've all experienced the grip of an agitated state during which we act out in undesirable ways; that's the grip of complex.) The most obvious example of this is the great likelihood that Trump never expected to get elected president—a most ironic "trick" that was played on him. Jung (1954) further describes the trickster:

> *The so-called civilized man has forgotten the trickster. He remembers him only figuratively and metaphorically, when, irritated by his own ineptitude, he speaks of fate playing tricks on him or of things being bewitched. He never suspects that his own hidden and apparently harmless shadow has qualities whose dangerousness exceeds his wildest dreams. As soon as people get together in masses and submerge the individual, the shadow is mobilized, and, as history shows, may even be personified and incarnated. (par. 478)*

At the time Jung was writing of the incarnation of evil that was wrought in Nazi Germany, led by Hitler. This archetype of evil not only possessed Hitler, but, because of the trust he engendered in the German people, was responsible for spreading a mass psychosis throughout German society. This huge inflation of the "Blond Beast," as Nietzsche named this dark shadow of the German psyche, resulted in the torture and slaughter of tens of millions of people over the next decade. This wasn't long ago, only two generations in our collective past. And it is chillingly similar to the mob feelings of fear, hate, and racism that Trump continues to invoke, with all his might, at his mass rallies.

The Trickster as Warning

Jung further claims that the trickster figure also dwells deep in our own individual subjective shadows. He states: "The shadow, although by definition a negative figure, sometimes has certain clearly discernable traits and associations which seem to point to a quite different background. It is as though it were hiding meaningful contents under an unprepossessing exterior." (par. 485)

From a psychological perspective, it's our own apathy, individually and collectively, that has constellated a compensating reaction from the collective unconscious. We have fallen into our own trickster shadow, an unconscious state, politically and morally. This came about by not paying attention to those left behind, socially and economically, over the last few decades. The liberal majority has also collectively pushed political correctness to sometimes unreasonable limits, suppressing our own darker attitudes.

Trump's election can be seen in psychological terms as a regression, a conscious attempt to turn back the clock and live life from a simpler perspective—a time when the United States was whiter, more European. That perhaps was a time that feels safer and more secure than the present for those most displaced. This point applies equally to the recent vote in Britain to leave the European Union, and is reflected in the rise of nationalism and the extreme political right in many other European countries and beyond, as previously mentioned.

But with Trump in America, possessed by the archetypal trickster, we have no idea what he'll do from one day to the next. And that is an exponentially greater danger in an unstable world.

On one level, what we are witnessing is a psychological split or dissociation between the right and the left. This split is between younger, well-educated, social liberals and slower adapting, older, and less educated social conservatives. The shrillest voices come from the most extreme on each side of the equation. The more strenuous their efforts, the greater the polarity produced. The tension between these opposites within both the American and global psyche is immense. Each side is clearly the shadow of the other. And evidence of this projection of the shadow onto the "other" abounds geopolitically.

In the United States, Trump and his cronies took full advantage of this ideological split. He preached a strong nationalistic and populist message, and capitalized on people's hate and fear—the inferior feelings in our collective culture. He did it so well that he got himself elected president, a most unlikely outcome, or so most of us thought, including professional pollsters. But now Trump has got us, even as the trickster has him.

Within this new dynamic, we must now confront the trickster as it manifests within him. It's a wake-up call and a warning as to what is going on in the shadow-lands of the American and global psyche. But while it's a clear and present danger to us, it's also an unprecedented opportunity to become more conscious of ourselves psychologically. This is the hidden meaning and value that the trickster brings to us.

The Repression of Truth

One of the most troubling aspects of the Trump administration is its irregular relationship with the truth. Trump and his acolytes always brand real news as "fake news" if they don't like it, and they speak bald lies that they insist are true. They will continue on repeating these lies, no matter that they have no facts to back them up. The trickster as "false and cunning" is apparent in everything they do. And if we can't agree on what the basic facts are, how can any middle ground be found to resolve any issue? As James Comey, former director of the FBI, stated "Our country is led by those who will lie about anything, backed by those who will believe anything, based on information from media sources who will say anything." (Twitter, May 23rd, 2019, as reported in the LA Times).

The trickster, however, doesn't want to compromise with the status quo; rather the trickster wants to destroy the existing political structure. It's important to understand that this feeling is right, psychologically speaking. The current political landscape has become corrupt, and the ruling principle it runs on—the greed and power of special interests—does need to be replaced. But not by the false national populism that Trump and company are selling, like snake-oil salesmen at a Depression-era religious revival.

Trump's method (if it can be called that) is just a cynical way to play people while raping them of any remaining wealth. The planned so-called repeal and replacement of Obama-care, which fortunately has so far not passed Congress, is the most cynical of these. The result would give wealthy people a huge tax break, while kicking tens of millions of poor and middle-class Americans off affordable health care. That's playing quite a trick on the people who voted for you and got you elected as president — a classic "bait and switch."

This dark shadow of Trump and his administration must be confronted and a genuine way found to address the real needs of "We, the people...." And while on one level the split is between liberals and conservatives in our society, the much larger and more serious split, I would argue, is between the wealthy one percent and the rest of us. What the wealthy one percent have managed to do — at least those on the radical right (Meyer, 2016) — is to use that liberal–conservative dichotomy to their advantage, in particular to convince unsuspecting conservative rural voters to support getting their candidates elected, even though those candidates consistently govern against their best interests.

What Trump and his new alt-right friends have accomplished is to raise this demagoguery to a new art form, using fearful and sometimes hateful nationalistic and populist rhetoric. This rhetoric sells very well right now in Middle America, but buyer's remorse may be just around the corner. It could be swift and ugly. Trump as trickster may be able to fool some of the people some of the time, but not all of the people all of the time, as P. T. Barnum once famously stated.

Mortificatio and Purificatio

Mortificatio and calcinatio are two terms that refer to the same operation of dealing with the nigredo, the dark shadow, which Trump represents in spades. This process is specifically related to the mercurial trickster archetype. Mortificatio literally means killing; Trump has efficiently killed off traditional politics in this country, by killing off the influence of the traditional Democratic and Republican parties and disregarding basic Constitutional requirements. The electorate had grown weary of both Democratic and Republican lawmakers who increasingly governed from an imperious attitude of entitlement. The Bush and Clinton "dynasties" had been ruling for most of the last three decades, and the electorate needed and wanted a change.

The exception came in the form of Barack Obama, who represented an unprecedented renewal of hope and change, but could only achieve so much in a toxic and divided Washington (read Mitch McConnell here) in his eight years in office; the passing of the Affordable Care Act was his greatest achievement. But having a forward-looking African American president was obviously too much change for many people to assimilate. Also, many formerly middle-class citizens were now falling behind economically, even as the top one percent racked up record earnings, bonuses, and wealth. Trump now seized the moment to peddle his politics of hate and fear, appealing to the lowest common denominator with false hope and a vacuous and false populist message.

The old king, as represented by Washington politics as usual, very much needed to die. So, psychologically speaking, a calcinatio did need to take place. Unfortunately, the calcinatio did not ensue following this mortification, as the change to Donald Trump has turned out to be a nightmare of immense proportions. His authoritarian approach to government is more neo-fascist than democratic, and he is said to run the White House like a Mafioso godfather. He admires and even exalts world leaders like

Vladimir Putin of Russia, Victor Orban of Hungary, and Kim Jong-un of North Korea, a trifecta of tyrannical despots. In the meantime, Trump attacks America's traditional allies, like France, Germany, and even Canada, its largest trading partner and ally since World War I.

As Madeline Albright stated (2018): "The United States has had flawed presidents before; in fact, we have never had any other kind, but we have not had a chief executive in the modern era whose statements and actions are so at odds with democratic ideals." Albright continues:

> ... we have reason to be concerned by the gathering array of political and social currents buffeting us right today—currents propelled by the dark underside of the technological revolution, the corroding effects of power, the American president's disrespect for truth, and the widening acceptance of dehumanizing insults, Islamophobia, and anti-Semitism as being within the bounds of normal public debate. We are not there yet, but these feel like signposts on the road back to an era when fascism found nourishment and individual tragedies were multiplied millions-fold. (p. 5)

To purify ourselves we will have to elect him out of office. This would be the cleanest way to rid ourselves of him, both psychologically and politically. But to do that there will have to be better choices available than the tired old "dynastic" thinking of the traditional Democratic and Republican parties. Hope has come in the way of the new women's movement constelled by Trump's win in 2016, and as manifested by the millions of women and men across the country who marched for women's rights the day after Trump's inauguration on January 21, 2017.

It was the largest single-day protest in U.S. history. The goal of these now annual marches is to advocate legislation and policies regarding tolerance, human rights and other issues, including women's rights, immigration reform, healthcare reform, reproductive rights, the environment, LGBTQ rights, racial equality, freedom of religion, and workers' rights. According to organizers, the goal was to "send a bold message to our new administration on their first day in office, and to the world that women's rights are human rights" (Wikipedia, 2018).

From the seeds of this "revolt" against Trump, and everything he stands for—fear, hate, anger, anti-immigration, anti-Semitism, racism, misogyny, nationalism, demagoguery, etc.—a record number of women ran for elected office in the mid-term elections in 2018. And of these over one hundred new female representatives have been elected to the American Congress. That, I would suggest, is what hope looks like going forward. A purging and calcinatio of our politics by getting rid of old fixated patriarchal ideals and replacing them with fresh vital feminine ideals, carrying a deeper moral and ethical sense, and the energy to get some meaningful legislative work accomplished for future generations.

In summary, the trickster archetype manifests now to show us how deep the split is within the American and global psyche: between moral and immoral perspectives, rich and poor, liberal and conservative. Though we'd rather not deal with it, we're charged with the tremendous task of healing this split, first within our own psyche, and then in the American and world psyche. Confronted with our own dark shadow, we have no choice but to assimilate it. If we continue simply projecting this shadow onto the "other" we risk becoming engulfed by it. Though it is a great crisis to confront, it also presents us with a tremendous opportunity for psychological growth and renewal. The trickster confronts us now with this sacred task.

CHAPTER THREE

Calcinatio: The Dark Fire
of Vladimir Putin

Men do not know what is at variance agrees with itself. It is an attunement of opposite tensions, like that of the bow and the lyre. The bow is called life but its work is death. Mortals are immortals and immortals are mortals, the one living the others' death and dying the others' life. For souls it is death to become water, for water death to become earth. But from the earth comes water, and from water, soul. All things are an exchange for fire, and fire for all things, like goods for gold and gold for goods. The way up and the way down are the same.

— HERACLITUS (LATE 6TH CENTURY BCE)

Jung (1954) defines enantiodromia as a "running counter to"; in the course of events, everything that exists turns into its opposite. From life comes death and from death, rebirth. He states further, "Just as the cosmos arose from the primal fire, so must it return once more to the same—a dual process running its measured course through vast periods of time, a drama eternally re-enacted as the ancient Greek philosopher Heraclitus stated above." (C.W. # 6, par. 708)

There can be no doubt that the liberal democracies of the West that established themselves following World War II in Europe and elsewhere are now under threat from an unconscious pull back towards the opposite perspective, that of tyranny. It is something that demagogues and predators like Putin, Trump, and Orban have a great animal instinct for. They knowingly stoke the embers of fear and hate in their basest populations, creating a toxic fire of discontent that is then weaponized and directed upon democratic institutions in their countries, including a free press, an impartial judicial system, and genuine and free elections. The definition of a demagogue according to Merriman-Webster is, "a leader who makes use of popular prejudices and false claims and promises in order to gain power."

As Garry Kasparov, former world chess-master and opposition leader in Russia wrote about Putin in his 2015 book Winter Is Coming (a title based on the ominous refrain that echoed through the seasons of Game of Thrones);

> The rise and fall of Russian democracy would make for a painfully short book. It took just eight short years for Russia to go from jubilant crowds celebrating the collapse of the Soviet Union in 1992 to the ascendance of former KGB agent Vladimir Putin to the presidency. Then it took Putin another eight years to corrupt or dismantle nearly every democratic element in the country—balance in the branches of government, fair elections, independent judiciary, a free media, and a civil society that could work with the government instead of living in fear of it. (p. 1)

Putin pulled this "sleight of hand" by allowing his first deputy prime minister, Dmitry Medvedev, to take over as president after Putin had served in that role for eight years. Then Putin promptly took over as deputy prime minister, effectively switching jobs with Medvedev in what Kasparov (2015, p. 2) describes as a graceful "pas de deux" over the grave of Russian democracy." Six years later Medvedev handed the presidency back to Putin after changing the constitution to allow for Putin to serve for two more terms of six years apiece. At this point they were barely hiding the fact that the Russian democracy was once again a dictatorship. The rigged elections held every six years simply pay lip service to an allusion of democracy that does not exist at any level in Russian society.

Kasparov (2015, p. 257) continues: "Putin's early themes of restoring the national pride and structure that were lost with the fall of the USSR have slowly run out of steam and been replaced by a toxic mixture of nationalism, belligerence, and hatred." By 2014, the increasingly depleted opposition movement, long treated with contempt and ridicule, had been rebranded in the Kremlin-dominated media as dangerous fifth columnists, or "national traitors," in the vile language frequently borrowed from the Nazis.

The West has been very slow to catch on to the fact that Putin has no interest whatsoever in developing an open democratic society in Russia. "Putin didn't care how something looked as long he knew nobody would act to stop him. The only image he cared about was looking tough at home, and blatantly ignoring the feeble complaints of western leaders only helped him in this regard." These complaints could be about another Russian journalist being killed; a foreign business company being pushed out of the country after losing its investment; or when gas and oil were continually being used as political weapons. Kasparov continues: "What needed to be asked was what sort of government would continue such behavior, and where such a government would end up. Putin's regime operated on an amoral scale, something entirely different from that of Western nations struggling to understand what was happening behind the medieval red walls of the Kremlin." (p. 159)

For several years after Putin rose to power in 2000, the West tried to integrate him and his gang into the democratic ideals of the West, but instead the opposite has happened. Putin has instead exported his mafia-style government, where he is the "godfather" to his oligarchic lieutenants and to other countries. What began as Russia's problem is now the world's problem.

As Putin has incarnated a twenty-first-century version of what a Russian czar is, overlooking a totally corrupt system, he also is fully engaged in undermining any democracy around him. As Kasparov (2015, p.161) explains:

The Kremlin was not changing its standards; it was impos-
ing them on the outside world. The mafia corrupts every-
thing it touches. Bartering in human rights begins to ap-
pear to be acceptable. As an added benefit, Putin and his cro-
nies received the stamp of legitimacy from Western leaders
and businesses while making those same leaders complicit
in their crimes.

Just before the national U.S. election in November 2016, American intelligence agencies, including the CIA and the FBI, concluded that Russia, at Putin's direction, had intervened using online tools to influence the American election in favor of the eventual winner, Donald Trump. The same efforts by Russia have been made over the last few years in almost every European election, including those of Britain, France, Spain, Poland, Hungary, the Czech Republic, Ukraine, and Georgia. Albright (2018, p. 164) states:

Methods include the theft and release of e-mails, the gen-
eration of phony documents, the use of disguised iden-
tities on Facebook, and the dissemination of fictitious and
sometimes libelous "news" stories that are then picked up
and splashed around on social media. When Russia is con-
fronted with these allegations, the response has been typ-
ical ... to categorically deny any role, then concoct a false
equivalency by accusing the West of doing the same thing.

The purpose of this is to "inflame public opinion" on both the right and the left and undermine the democracy of each individual country, one government at a time. As Madeline Albright points out (2018, p. 165): "This agenda is not ideological; it is about power, pure and simple."
Edinger (1985) relates that in the The Twelve Keys of Basil

Valentine, a 15th-century alchemist, there is the following alchemical recipe for calcinatio: "Take a fierce grey wolf, which … is found in the valleys and mountains of the world, where he roams almost savage with hunger. Cast him entirely to the ashes in a great fire. By this process the king will be liberated; and when it has been performed thrice the lion has overcome the wolf, and will find nothing more to devour in him. Thus our body has been rendered fit for the first stage of the work" (p. 18). Edinger continues:

> *Psychologically, it would signify the death of the ruling principle of consciousness, the highest authority in the hierarchal structure of the ego. Death of the king would thus be accompanied by a regressive dissolution of the conscious personality. This course of events is indicated by the fact that the body of the king is fed to a ravening wolf; that is, the ego has been devoured by hungry desirousness. The wolf in turn is fed to the fire. But wolf = desire and desire = fire. Thus, desirousness consumes itself. After a descent into hell, the ego (king) is reborn, phoenix like, in a purified state. (p.19)*

The dissolution of the ruling principle of democracy is being felt and witnessed every day now in the United States and around the globe. This is in large part due to how wildly successful Vladimir Putin (with his wolfish desires) was in helping to get Donald Trump elected. This is likely an outcome Putin never dreamed possible, just as Trump likely never imagined he would actually be elected president. Trump is now Putin's "operative," undermining democracy in the United States and around the world each and every day. The damage to the United States and the world's democracies is incalculable as Trump takes America down a rocky and chaotic road of regressive nationalism, protectionism, and isolation from the rest of the world.

In this deteriorating process the United States is abdicating its role as the model for world democracies. In its stead the two totalitarian regimes of Russia and China are filling the void left by America, along with their toxic and tyrannical methods of government.

Trump, even after his own intelligence agencies had excoriated Russia for meddling in the 2016 election, has said nary a negative word about Putin, but rather talks in admiration of him as a very strong leader who is admired by his people. It is not clear from the Mueller investigation results whether Putin has Trump in a bind with compromising information about him. But it is a psychological fact that Trump behaves as if Putin has compromising information about him.

The former KGB agent Putin would know several ways to have put Trump into a compromised position, beginning with the temptation of having a Trump Tower built in Moscow. This is something Trump has wanted for over three decades now, and was actively seeking with Russia right up until the election in November of 2016. Allegations that the Trump Organization has "laundered" Russian oligarchs' money through its channels over at least two decades are also part of the ongoing investigation. In the meantime, Trump is receiving open support from Russia and Putin, while challenging the status quo within his own country, and attacking the democratic institutions of NATO, the United Nations, and the European Union. All have served as a bulwark against totalitarianism for the past seventy years. All the while Trump is trying to subvert the justice system, openly attacks the free press on a daily basis, and lies to anyone and everyone when it suits him to do so. He has been described as a professional liar by some of his own cabinet members. (Woodward, 2018, p. 338)

Edinger (1985) describes some of the biblical images of calcinatio, which includes a story about Nebuchadnezzar's fiery furnace. He commanded everyone to fall down and worship his golden image. Shadrach, Meshach, and Abednego refused. Nebuchadnezzar had them thrown into the fiery furnace, but they remained unharmed. Nebuchadnezzar's rage can be compared to the fiery furnace. Edinger (1985) continues: "He [Nebuchadnezzar] personifies the power motive, the arbitrary authority of the inflated ego that undergoes calcinatio when its overwhelming pretensions are frustrated by the presence of a transpersonal authority (the God of Shadrach, Meshach, and Abednego)" (p. 23 – 24). Nebuchadnezzar also corresponds to the king in the alchemical recipe who is "fed to the wolf" and then calcined.

Edinger suggests that Nebuchadnezzar's furnace represents an archetypal situation wherein if one challenges an arbitrary authority, one will survive only if one approaches it from the attitude of the Self as opposed to the ego. With democracy currently under assault and so many ultra-right-wing nationalist leaders in power, seeking to undermine public confidence in our elections, the courts, and the media, one could say that the tyrannical spirit of Nebuchadnezzar is alive and thriving for the moment. The question is, does the West have the courage to stand up to these tyrannical leaders, such as Putin, Orban, and Trump as Shadrach, Meshach, and Abednego stood up to Nebuchadnezzar?

Psychologically, the rise and possible fall of democracy exemplifies the archetype of death and rebirth, a cycle that repeats itself continuously throughout human history. After seventy-five years of post–World War II expansion of democracy, culminating with the fall of the "Berlin Wall" in 1989 and the dissolution of the Soviet Union, that old ruling principle is dissolving. For the moment it seems as if a push towards "illiberal democracies" is taking place—which is just a new twist on what totalitarian states look like today. That is, such states are nominally democratic, run highly controlled predetermined elections, and otherwise act like any former authoritarian state. In Russia this includes preaching fear and hatred of outsiders to the base electorate, controlling and silencing (even murdering) the media, absorbing the judicial branch of government within the executive branch, and creating an oligarchic class of individuals who are beholding to the leader of the state. And if any Russian oligarch chooses to oppose Putin, he will be jailed, shot, or poisoned.

The ruling principle of tyranny likely cannot sustain itself in the long run psychologically, if only because it will burn itself out from within by its own toxic elements, following the maxim that hate corrodes the container in which it is kept. This is evidenced by the dissolution of the Soviet Union in 1989, where the empire literally imploded from within under its own weight of corruptness and ineptness. But the struggle to preserve democracy in part will be difficult because democracies are not, by nature, set up to defend themselves against outside adversaries. As Revel (1983, p. 4) points out:

> *Totalitarianism liquidates its internal enemies or smashes opposition as soon as it arises; it uses methods that are simple and infallible because they are undemocratic. But democracy can defend itself only very feebly; its internal enemy has an easy time of it because he exploits the right to disagree that is inherent in democracy ... those seeking to destroy democracy appear to be fighting for legitimate aims, while its defenders are pictured as repressive reactionaries.*

Edinger relates that the 16th century mystic Joseph Boehme describes in his writings two "trees of fire," the fire of the Holy Spirit and the fire of God's wrath. He reflects that the tree of life as a tree of fire alludes to the passage in Genesis (3:24,RSV): "He drove out the man; and at the east of the garden of Eden he placed the cherubim, and a flaming sword which turns in every way, to guard the way to the tree of life.... The Zohar says the flaming sword symbolizes the trials with which God overwhelms man, that he may be restored to the way of goodness." (p. 35)

We can state with certainty that, at this moment in history, the liberal democracies of the West are being overwhelmed by the ideology of the illiberal democracies of the world, led by corrupt and power hungry leaders such as Putin, Orban, and now Trump. Soon it will be time to firmly stand up to them—and a conflagration is likely unavoidable.

The ruling principle of tyranny, as opposed to democracy, is now in ascendency three short decades after the fall of Communism and the Soviet Union. The movement against democracy over that period has been quietly taking place almost unnoticed as mere challenges to the status quo that seem very legitimate in themselves. But make no mistake, we are now again at a crucial inflection point when democracies all over the world are under the direct threat of being undermined, often from an enemy within. The question now is how all of this will play out in reality.

Psychologically, we have two great fires that are burning now. One fire is that of truth and democracy and freedom—the fire of the Holy Spirit. The second fire is that of tyranny—made up of hatred, fear, corruption, and injustice; the fire of the God of Wrath. We are now at a time in the world's history reminiscent of the 1930s, when fascist governments sprang up in several European countries, including Spain, Italy, and Germany, prior to World War II. Could it be that the firestorms of hell that exploded at that time will turn the world once again into an inferno of death and suffering?

We are just beginning to gauge the seriousness of the situation, just beginning to measure the depth of the powerful forces of tyranny in our midst, constellating all around us now. A cleansing fire may be what is required, but the price we will pay to rid ourselves of this encroaching tyranny will only increase as time passes and freedoms the world over are curtailed.

CHAPTER FOUR

Solutio: Brexit and the Dismemberment of Great Britain

It is incredible to watch Great Britain, which once occupied more than 20 percent of the earth's landmass, moving ever closer to the brink of its own disintegration.

— JAMES KIRCHICK (2017, 162)

In many ancient texts solutio is reported as the most important alchemical operation. Just as calcinatio deals with the element of fire, so solutio deals with the element of water. "Water was thought of as the womb and solutio as a return to the womb for rebirth.... In many creation myths, water is the original material out of which the world was created" (Edinger, 1985). One alchemical recipe for solutio is the following:

> Dissolve then sol and luna in our dissolving water, which is familiar and friendly, and the next in nature unto them, and as it were a womb, a mother, an original, the beginning and the end of their life. And that is the very reason why they are meliorated or amended in this water, because like nature rejoiceth in like nature.... Thus it behooves you to join consanguinity, or sameness of kind.... And because sol and luna have their origin from this water their mother; it is necessary therefore that they enter into it again, to wit, into their mother's womb, that they may regenerate or born again, and made more healthy, more noble and more strong.

(p. 48)

In Jungian analysis, if all goes well, the old hard attitudes of each analysand are broken down, softened up, and subsequently dissolved. Through an oftentimes arduous and lengthy process, the old attitudes are finally melted down and recast into better adaptive, more holistic attitudes, and thus transformed. This is achieved by incrementally tapping into the wisdom of the unconscious via dreams and active imagination, and the individual's assimilation of this wisdom into his or her conscious attitude.

In Britain, on the fateful day of June 23, 2016, the electorate saw fit to dissolve their relationship with the European Union by voting to leave it by a 52–48% vote—this, despite the warnings and objections of the British Prime Minister, the majority of the members of British Parliament, the Governor of the Bank of England, the heads of British Intelligence, the North Atlantic Treaty Organization, and the International Monetary Fund. The tumult that has resulted from this fateful vote has provoked a crisis in the country and across Europe, and the bad news may be only just beginning. Kirchich (2017) states:

> Approval of "Brexit," the portmanteau adopted to describe this less that amicable separation, immediately plunged the United Kingdom into political, economic, and social crises. Within hours of the vote result, Prime Minister David Cameron announced his intention to resign, setting off a Conservative Party leadership race to succeed him. Several days later, Labour MPs overwhelming passed a motion of non-confidence against their leader Jeremy Corbyn, furious that he had barely lifted a finger to assist the "Remain" campaign. Acknowledging that businesses and households would indefinitely delay spending and investment in the face of such profound economic uncertainty, Bank of England governor Mark Carney warned of "economic post-

traumatic stress disorder." The Economic Intelligence Unit, meanwhile, warned of a 6 percent contraction in GDP by 2020 and increasing unemployment. Britain's AAA credit rating, which it had enjoyed since 1978, was downgraded to AA. After only a week in post-Brexit Britain, police logged a 500 percent increase in hate crimes, with everyone from long-resident Cypriots to native born black Britons reporting abuse at the hands of freshly emboldened English nationalists.... Beyond all these tangible aftershocks, a deep an ineffable sense of unease set in among many Britons, particularly younger ones, who had voted overwhelming to stay within the EU. At risk was their future conception of themselves as Europeans, along with the benefits that identity accrues, not the least of which are the "four freedoms" they had long taken for granted: the free movement of goods, services, persons, and capital across the union. (p. 154)

It is true that Great Britain, as an island nation, has always been more independent than its European neighbors, and always viewed the EU more as a practical way to gain access to a free market to sell its goods, as opposed to supporting the EU's wider political purposes, of which it has always been suspicious. Even so, the stark reality is that Britons were manipulated and lied to in the process leading up to the fateful vote, and sold a bill of rotten goods.

The situation only became possible when the then Prime Minister, Conservative leader David Cameron, in 2015, after being elected, acquiesced to the extreme right-wing members of his own party and agreed to have a national referendum on EU membership—a vote he never dreamed he could lose, until he did.

The opposition charge was led in the first place by Nigel Farage, a former London banker and leader of England's UKIP (United Kingdom Independence Party), whose xenophobic speeches in the European Parliament for many years prior are legendary, though not in the least truthful. Farage's rantings were retold by Britain's tabloid press, thus influencing many in the country. In a judicial investigation into the truthfulness of British media in 2009, a former Blair aide, Alastair Campbell said this:

> *If the Eurosceptic press is to believed, Britain is going to be forced to unite as a single country with France, Church schools are being forced to hire atheist teachers, Scotch whisky is being classified as inflammable liquid, British soldiers must take orders in French, the price of chips is being raised by Brussels, Europe is insisting on one size fits all condoms, new laws are being proposed on how to climb a ladder, it will be a criminal offense to criticize Europe, Number 10 (Downing Street) must fly the European flag, and finally Europe is brainwashing our children with pro-European propaganda! (as cited in Kirchick, 2017, p.156)*

Boris Johnson, the former London mayor, and now Prime Minister, also has blood on his hands from the vote. He decided to join the "Leave" campaign just shortly before the vote, a cynical decision on his part, as he had never pronounced anything more than a mild Eurosceptic view previously. But expecting a "Remain" victory, he saw his new position as a way to reinforce his favor with the "Leave" constituents of the Conservative party, positioning himself for a run at Prime Minister after the "Remain" vote had taken place. This seemed to be a miscalculation on his part, which originally cost him a lot of political capital; but the subsequent resignation of Teresa May as Conservative leader and Prime Minister has now allowed Johnson to take her place.

Ultimately, it was Farage and the UKIP party's argument to return to a "Little England" that put the Brexit vote over the top. A nationalist promise, not unlike Trump's message to the electorate in the United States, to magically return to a whiter, safer time in society, when people had more supposed control over their lives. Kirchick (2017, p. 171) reports:

According to researchers Matthew Goodwin and Robert Ford, UKIP voters can be characterized as losers in the new economy. "Left behind" by automation and the exporting of jobs overseas. They support UKIP not for any particular economic policies it espouses, but because it promises to re-vivify a lost Britain in which they were more valued, one that would include drastically less immigration.

It should be pointed out that strains arisen over immigration and that more than a million Central and Eastern Europeans have come to live in Britain since the expansion of the EU member-ship in 2004. But Britain could have invoked an EU limit on these numbers if it had wished. Unfortunately, it did not think the numbers of people immigrating to Britain would be much lower —a calculation then Prime Minister Tony Blair clearly fumbled. Countering a negative narrative on immigration, a 2014 study found the following:

European migrants to the United Kingdom make an annual net fiscal contribution of 20 billion pounds and that more than 60 percent of the migrants from Western and South-ern Europe are university graduates (compared to only 24 percent of UK-born workers). To replace this level of human imported "capital," the United Kingdom would have to spend 6.8 billion pounds on education annually. (Kirchick, 2017, p. 169)

The British nostalgia for former times is an interesting phenomenon to consider from a psychological perspective. Neumann (1954, as cited in Edinger) tells us:

Many forms of nostalgia and longing signify no more than a return to uroboric incest and self-dissolution, from the unio mystica of the saint to the drunkard's craving for unconsciousness, and the death-romanticism of the Germanic races. The incest we term "uroboric" is self-surrender and regression. It is the form of incest taken by the infantile ego that creeps back to the mother and has not yet come to itself; but the sick ego of the neurotic can also take this form and so can a later, exhausted ego that creeps back to the mother after having found fulfillment. (p. 49)

Psychologically speaking, the majority of the British electorate was seduced into a "Leave" vote based upon the lies of Farage and Johnson and as was promulgated expertly on social media by Cambridge Analytica, the data management firm that identified three million voters who normally didn't vote at all in British elections. These three million new-found voters were then targeted through social media with catch phrases such as "Take back control," which evoked their deeply held beliefs about the European Union and how it was negatively affecting their lives.

The actual facts are quite different, however. No less than thirty-two reports commissioned by the British Foreign Ministry, summing up over 2,300 research articles studying Britain and the EU, found that there was overwhelming evidence that Britain benefited from being a member of the EU, and further that there were no significant drawbacks. As Kirchick reports (2017, p. 166):

The clearest rationale is economic. Forty-five percent of British exports are sold to fellow members of the EU, supporting some three million jobs. Once outside the EU, Britain would lose preferential access to the Common Market and be forced to sign a new trade agreement with the bloc

bound to be on less favorable terms than its current ar-
rangement.

Recent evidence indicates that the funds to pay for Cambridge Analytica may have been provided by Robert Mercer, the American billionaire IT mogul who was invested in the company and who also happened to be the largest campaign contributor to Donald Trump's U.S. election campaign. There is also now email evidence that Steve Bannon, in 2015, who was then working for Cambridge Analytica and who eventually worked as an advisor in the Trump White House, had helped set up the Cambridge Analytica office in Britain. Around the same time Bannon was also setting up an American office for Cambridge Analytica in Alexandria, Virginia, across the Potomac River from Washington, D.C., to carry out oppositional data research for the Trump campaign.

Email evidence from 2015 was unearthed that links Bannon to Brittany Kaiser, the director of program development at Cambridge Analytica, and to Arron Banks, who headed the Leave.EU campaign, and contributed a reported nine million pounds to the effort. A 2018 article in the New Yorker Magazine by Jane Meyer states:

Whether foreign funds secretly supported the Brexit movement has become the focus of intense speculation and investigation in the U.K. The British probes, in many respects, are parallel to the Robert Mueller investigation of possible Russian support for Trump's 2016 campaign. Banks has drawn particular scrutiny because his business spent some nine million pounds supporting the Brexit campaign, making him the country's single largest political-campaign donor by far, despite questions about whether he had the personal wealth to contribute that much on his own. Banks has insisted that his contributions were legal, and that foreign sources, including Russia, contributed no funds. But multiple British agencies have launched inquiries, in-

cluding a criminal investigation into Banks's role by the National Crime Agency, the U.K.'s equivalent to the F.B.I. (online)

This is also evidence, then, that the level of psychological deception and the seduction of the lies perpetuated by the "Leave Campaign" were much deeper than previously realized and that much of the public was completely fooled by them. The article goes on to state:

> *The possibility that both Brexit and the Trump campaign simultaneously relied upon the same social-media company and its transgressive tactics, as well as some of the same advisers, to further far-right nationalist campaigns, set off alarm bells on both sides of the Atlantic. The Mueller type investigation in Britain will investigate to see just how deep these ties may be between Mercer, Bannon and the Brexit campaign. Further they will investigate whether there were any ties between the Leave campaign and Wiki-Leaks and Julian Assange, the possible link between the Russian hacking of the Democratic Party computers and the Trump campaign. (Meyer, 2018, online)*

Damian Collins, a member of the British Parliament and chair of its Digital, Culture, Media and Sport Committee, states that the new emails:

> *. . . suggest that the role of Bannon and Mercer is far deeper and more complex than we realized. There's a big question about whether Mercer's money was used in the Brexit campaign and it absolutely underscores why Britain needs a proper Mueller-style investigation. There are direct links between the political movements behind Brexit and Trump. We've got to recognize the bigger picture here. This is being*

coordinated across national borders by very wealthy people
in a way we haven't seen before. (as quoted in Meyer, 2018,
online)

Whatever the outcome of the American and British investigations, it is clear that the movement toward nationalist populist radical right-wing politics is a worldwide phenomenon. And the startling fact is that it is now threatening liberal democracies everywhere. The fact that it may be coordinated by the likes of radical right-wing billionaires like Mercer and Trump in the United States, Banks, Murdock, and Farage in Britain, and billionaire oligarchs along with Putin in Russia is chilling.

Turning back to our alchemical symbolism, solutio is often performed on the king who is drowning. One text has the drowning king say: "Whosoever will free me from the waters and lead me to dry land, him I will prosper with ever-lasting riches" (Jung, CW#12, par. 434). Edinger (1981) tells us that psychologically the meaning of this is that the old ruling principle, the drowning king, is being resolved and passing away. The question is, what will the new ruling principle be that takes shape, that coagulates, alchemically speaking, and replaces the old ruling principle? The threat to liberal democracies being replaced by tyranny on a global level is very real right now.

Will these illiberal democracies replace our liberal democracies? Arguably, this has already happened in countries such as Poland and Hungary, where one party rule is being restored and opposition parties are being largely eliminated or manipulated by the ruling party. In the meantime the press is under attack, the courts answer to the ruling party, as opposed to being a separate branch of government, and democratic protests are snuffed out in short order.

Circling back to Britain, leaving the EU is perhaps just the first step in its unraveling as a major Western power for the last five hundred years. Scotland had already held a vote on independence in 2014, wherein the citizenry narrowly voted to remain within

Great Britain. The reason the Scottish citizens did not choose to leave at that time was because they were, as part of Britain, also part of the European Union. Now that Britain as a whole has chosen to leave the EU, this reasoning no longer applies. The Scottish electorate itself chose to remain in the EU by a 62:38% ratio in the Brexit vote, posting a "Remain" win in all of its thirty-two counties.

Scotland's first minister, Nicola Sturgeon, has stated that it is "democratically unacceptable that Scotland faced the prospect of leaving the EU against its will" and that a second independence referendum is "highly likely" after the UK voted to leave the EU. Indeed the preparations to enable a second vote have now been implemented in the Scottish legislature, and a two-year process has now begun to ready the people for a second referendum. Thus it appears Britain's leaving the European Union could well have unintended consequences in dismembering the United Kingdom as a whole.

In the meantime, Britain's extraction of itself from the EU has been so debilitating and excruciating that other EU nations are not likely to join them anytime soon, despite Nigel Farage and UKIP hoping that this would be the case. But the economic and political damage to Britain may be only just beginning. In addition, Britain's withdrawal from European affairs will certainly weaken the European Union and embolden other dictatorships, such as Russia and China, to behave even more aggressively in the region.

Thus two of the world's great democracies, the United States and Britain, within the space of just a few years, have unhitched themselves from 75 years of a pro-European stance that arguably has prevented much conflict while supporting peace and prosperity globally.

The results of this dissolution of relationship between the United States, Britain, and the European Union is unknown. In alchemy, after a solutio comes a new coagulatio. But we have no idea what will coalesce in its place. We do know, however, that these dissolutions were both regressive in nature and largely based upon the seductive lies of nationalist populist leaders like Nigel Farage and Boris Johnson in England and Donald Trump in the U.S. And the fact that there is a clear link between the two through Robert Mercer and Cambridge Analytica and likely Wiki-Leaks and Russian government hackers under Vladimir Putin, should give us all cause to again be alert. Edinger (1985) reminds us that solutio is often experienced as dismemberment and fragmentation as opposed to containment.

Undoubtedly, a majority of the British electorate were seduced by the lies put to them by individuals like Farage and Johnson and others like Bannon and Mercer who lust for power at any cost. Now Britain has been dismembered because of its collective lack of psychological maturity, though we don't know the full extent of this yet. Great Britain could well become just Little England again very soon. This is not an outcome that was well thought through before the precipitous and crooked vote to leave. It is a hard lesson the nation is now learning.

CHAPTER FIVE

Separatio: Germany and the United States; Rethinking NATO

Eris, Goddess of Discord and sister of Ares, presides over separatio. It was she who came uninvited to a marriage on Olympus and flung into the midst of the gathering an apple inscribed "to the fairest." Thus she brought about the judgment of Paris. Comparisons are odious and comparison is what the golden apple provoked. To determine what is "more" and what is "most" requires and leads to judgments. Such actions disturb the status quo and generate conflict, but they may lead to greater consciousness.

— KIRK & RAVEN (AS CITED IN EDINGER, 1985, PP. 193–194)

A nd so, it was that Paris, an unwitting and lowly shepherd, was forced to make a judgment of governing values among power, knowledge, and beauty as represented respectively by Hera, Athena, and Aphrodite. This was an act of separatio, which thus led him to another stage of development through conflict. Fortunately or unfortunately, there is a state of conflict presently between Germany and the United States.

True, this conflict had been simmering for years, based upon the fact that the United States has had tens of thousands of troops stationed there since the end of World War II in 1945. Seventy-five years later, this is clearly getting old for many Germans, who would prefer not to be a launching pad for American missiles aimed at Russia. In fact, most Germans prefer a policy of "neutrality" between the United States and Russia, despite the fact it is illogical to assume that there ever could be a state of neutrality between a democratic nation (the United States) and a totalitarian nation (Russia), which is consistently focused on disrupting any and all democracies, including those of Germany and the United States.

Trust of the German people in the United States was shaken greatly in 2013 by Edward Snowden, a former National Security Agency contractor for the United States, when he revealed documents showing how much surveillance information was being compiled by the National Security Agency (NSA) about the German population. Adding to the insult was that the German foreign intelligence gathering service, the Bundesnachrichtendienst (BND), was complicit with the NSA in these operations, including the apparent monitoring of German Chancellor Angela Merkel's cell phone conversations.

While Snowden is commonly regarded as a hero today in Germany for making these revelations, it now seems rather obvious that he was, wittingly or unwittingly, working for the Russians as one of Putin's "puppets." This is substantiated by the fact that Moscow has provided him asylum in Russia, a highly unusual move for them, unless you consider that he was all along a Russian "asset." Kirchick (2017) states:

> More likely is that Snowden, consciously or unconsciously, arrived in Russia as a result of an operation controlled by Moscow via "cut-outs," espionage parlance for mutually trusted interlocutors who may or may not know the ultimate purpose they're serving. No government, least of all the Russian Federation, grants asylum to a "walk-in" (an agent from a foreign intelligence service who literally walks into another country's diplomatic post promising to spill the beans) a mere month after encountering him". (p. 73)

Further damning to Snowden is that he did not limit his leaks to the information that the NSA was collecting just on Americans, but began leaking information on what the NSA was collecting against foreign enemy powers, such as Russia and China.

At this point he became a "defector, if not a traitor," according to Kirchick (2017). Kirchick continues: "Irrespective of his initial intentions, Snowden has been an FSB (the new Russian KGB) asset from the moment he landed in Moscow, where his revelations, released in drip-drip fashion, have been carefully calibrated to ensure maximum damage to western interests". (p. 75)

Snowden's "dump" included releasing information about Russian NSA surveillance that may have tipped off the Russians to the fact that they had to alter some of their systems of communication in order to go undetected. This was likely a factor in Russia's ability to avoid detection while they invaded and annexed Crimea in 2014, and likewise on their movements when they invaded Ukraine in the same year. As these were the first two invasions on the European continent by a foreign power since World War II, their significance cannot be overstated.

Snowden's actions may also have helped in the formation of ISIS (Islamic State of Iraq and the Levant). According to Michael Morrell, a former CIA agent, "Within weeks of the leaks, terrorist organizations around the world were already starting to modify their actions in light of what Snowden disclosed. Communication sources dried up, tactics were changed" (as cited in Kirchick, 2017, p. 75). Kirchick further reports that "after the November 2015 attack in Paris by homegrown jihadists took the lives of 130 people, The EU counterterrorism coordinator said the Snowden's revelations had helped the terrorists avoid detection". (p. 75 - 76)

Still, it was the monitoring of Merkel's phone calls, apparently over a ten-year period, which enraged Germans and very much damaged relations between Germany and the United States. This led an investigation of the NSA's work by the German Parliament, and the eventual expulsion of the CIA station chief in Berlin. Curiously, no other foreign country's surveillance operations were investigated, only the United States. This, in spite of ongoing reports of Russia continuously hacking into their political computer systems in order to effect democratic German elections.

Subsequently, most of the charges of espionage against the United States, including the monitoring of Merkel's phone calls, could not be proved. But the damage to the relationship between the two countries had already occurred. This was all accomplished once again by the Fire-Sower-in-Chief, Vladimir Putin. Separating former countries that had been friendly with each other, like Germany and the United States, is central to Putin's overall strategy to divide and conquer.

Still, there are very good reasons for the CIA to be collecting surveillance in Germany, including defending against Al-Qaeda and ISIS and the known existence of Russian spies within the German BND. Kirchick (2017) further states:

> It seemed never to have crossed the minds of the outraged German press and public that a substantial portion of American spying in Germany has been directed not at their government but at adversarial powers like China and Russia.... One hopes that the heads of German intelligence agencies would be appalled to hear about their agents chummily consorting with an accomplice of Edward Snowden, revealing to her the operational details of an ally's clandestine activities. (p.79)

German Reunification and Russian Revisionism

A significant part of the equation today in Germany is a Russian revisionism of the past. It begins with the oddly held belief by the majority of Germans that the reunification of East and West Germany was a "gift" from Russia coming out of the Cold War. It is true that Mikhail Gorbachev did decide to allow the Warsaw Pact to dismantle peacefully, but only after the United States, pursuing a rigorous anti-Communist agenda, forced a beleaguered USSR into bankruptcy as it was attempting to equal the U.S. in a decade's-long arms race—a race that the USSR could never have won.

This convenient piece of amnesia about how the Cold War ended allows for a much more generous foreign policy towards Russia than it deserves. It also enables Germany to pursue a policy of impartiality and balance towards the East (Russia) and the

West (the EU and the U.S.) despite the fact that it is a policy founded upon a false premise. Russia, for its part, takes full advantage of this false equivalency to push the limits of its political influence in the region. According to Green Party Bundestag member Marie-Louise Beck:

> *A not insignificant portion of the German elite and public have deliberately buried their heads in the sand about Russia's activities in Ukraine and its aggression more generally, so terrified are they of the consequences that admitting the truth may entail "not wanting to know provides an opportunity for equidistance" between East and West, she says. There exists in Germany a "fear and fascination" with Putin, whose propagandists in the Kremlin know us better, our sensibilities better, than we know ourselves. (as cited in Kirchick, 2017, p. 106)*

Further, when NATO's Supreme Allied Commander, General Philip Breedlove, released evidence of military involvement in Ukraine—a heavily documented fact that Berlin, along with other European capitals, has been loath to admit—anonymous German government sources told Der Speigal that Breedlove was spreading "dangerous propaganda."

The reality is that Germans, seventy-five years after the end of World War II, are still horrified at the prospects of any nearby war. And Russia, for its part, understands this fear and exploits it to its benefit. As Kirchick (2017) explains it:

> *Moscow's cynical exploitation of World War II, a potent feature in its disinformation war against the West, has been orchestrated largely for a German audience. According to an early Kremlin narrative, the Maiden revolution and the government it brought to power in Kiev were not the achievements of ordinary Ukrainians fed up with corrup-*

*tion and mis-management, but the work of "Nazis" intent
on eradicating ethnic Russians and Jews.... In the parlance
of the Kremlin and its western sympathizers, "Nazi" does
not denote an admirer of German National Socialism so
much as it does an opponent of Russian foreign policy. (p.
104)*

This cynical revisionist historical perspective that Putin
serves up is ingested by a culpable German population because
it is very convenient for the people to think so. And this is precisely the effect Putin was intending. The specter of World War
III is just too terrifying for Germans to comprehend, and their
guilt about it just too great. Therefore, they will psychologically
repress—or better stated, actively suppress—these fears by agree-
ing with Putin about why he is behaving so badly in Crimea and
the Ukraine.

It was the Nazis that precipitated the death of 75 million
people across the globe from 1935–1945. But for Putin it simply doesn't matter, and he will brand anyone a Nazi who op-
poses him, anyone who is at all anti-Russian. That's a very dis-
honest but powerful re-interpretation of past European history,
if you are willing to believe it. Thus Putin exhibits a very keen
psychological understanding of his opponents. He then uses this
understanding to exploit the weaknesses of his opponents—the
German population, in this instance. Thus he acts like the true
predator and malignant narcissist that he unmistakably is.

The reality is that this suppression of the truth imposed upon
the German people themselves is actually pushing the situation
to an eventual crisis of much larger proportion down the road,
when Putin will finally cross a red line, perhaps in the Baltic states of Latvia, Estonia, and Lithuania, where there are still
many Russian nationals. This action, of course, would provide the
same pretense as Crimea and Georgia for Putin to invade, but it
would also likely trigger a response from NATO.

It is understandable that Germany wants to remain neutral,

but it is also very naïve, because Putin knows this very well, and is simply using it against not just Germany's best interests but the interests of the entire EU, NATO, and democracy in general. The former KGB officer knows how to enact this geopolitical strategy very well. The psychopathology of the German collective culture is being showcased today as much as it has been in the past. In the 1930s Hitler engendered a mass psychosis within the German collective by selling them on the idea that Germany could be great again; they just had to ignite a world war to claim back their living space and of course wipe out the Jewish population, and other undesirable groups, in the process—those "inferior" groups apparently being the greatest obstruction to making Germany great again.

Now in 2019, another psychosis is being engendered within the German collective, only this time it is being produced by Vladimir Putin, who is every bit a manipulator of the human psyche as Hitler was, and whose ultimate aim may not be too different. For Putin it is Russia against the world, just as it was Germany against the world in Hitler's 1930s. And it is under the guise of the victim that the bully goes to work. Mapping out the last few years with Putin attacking Georgia, Crimea, and the Ukraine, while waging cyber warfare against Germany, many other EU countries, and the United States, with the intention of affecting democratically held elections. If the effect he had on the 2016 American election is any measure of this strategy, Putin has succeeded beyond his wildest dreams. Having done so, we are naïve to think he will stop his aggressions any time soon. As Kirchick (2017) summarizes:

> Frequent allusions to Ukrainian Nazism are designed to remind Germans of their historical debt to Russia, and their intended effect on German attitudes is similar to that engendered by Ostpolitik (Eastpolitics). Accentuating Russian victimhood benefits Russians and Germans alike: It gives Germans license to disregard any obligations they might

feel (or, in the case of the NATO charter, actually have) to Central and Eastern Europe, and it lets Russia behave with impunity. By tarring Ukrainians as Nazis, Russia offers Germany a chance to atone for its past by joining a new popular front against fascism". (P. 104)

That's quite a "front" for Putin, a bully and a tyrant, selling tyranny and calling it atonement to gullible German and Russian populations.

The Threat to NATO

Added to the Snowden affair and Russian revisionism, we now have President Trump, seemingly another of Putin's "puppets," decrying that NATO is obsolete and that the United States should withdraw from the alliance. A January 2019 article in the New York Times by Julian Barnes and Helen Cooper reported that Trump had said privately on numerous occasions in 2018 that he wanted the United States to withdraw from NATO because it was expensive and he didn't see the point of it. He also chastised members of the twenty-nine-country federation who were not paying their fair share of expenses to run it (2% of their GDP). This, despite the fact that European nations have now contributed 100 billion dollars more to NATO in the last four years, predating Trump's time in office (NPR, April, 2019). The article further stated that "There are few things that President Vladimir V. Putin of Russia desires more than the weakening of NATO, the military alliance among the United States, Europe and Canada that has deterred Soviet and Russian aggression for 70 years." (online)

There was apparently fear at the 2018 NATO Alliance Summit meeting that Trump would create a fiasco by criticizing the agreement, and it was only some backroom scrambling by then defense secretary General Jim Mattis, a former NATO supreme allied commander, and then national security advisor John Bolton, that kept American support for the alliance on track. It is generally agreed among allies that a withdrawal from the NATO alliance would "drastically reduce Washington's influence in Europe and could embolden Russia for decades." (Barnes & Cooper, 2019, on-line)

Michael Flournay, former undersecretary of defense under President Barack Obama, said that any move to withdraw from the alliance, formed in 1949, "would be one of the most damaging things that any president could do to U.S. interests. It would destroy 70-plus years of painstaking work across multiple administrations, Republican and Democratic, to create perhaps the most powerful and advantageous alliance in history. And it would be the wildest success that Vladimir Putin could dream of" (Barnes & Cooper, 2019, on-line). Further, retired Adm. James G. Stavridis, another former supreme allied commander of NATO, said an American withdrawal from the alliance would be "a geopolitical mistake of epic proportion." The New York Times further reported that "the president's repeatedly stated desire to withdraw from NATO is raising new worries among national security officials amid growing concern about Mr. Trump's efforts to keep his meetings with Mr. Putin secret from even his own aides and an FBI investigation into the administration's ties to Russia." (Barnes & Cooper, 2019, on-line)

Psychologically speaking there are again historical and symbolic similarities with the myth of Paris. Edinger (1985) continues this story by telling us that the alchemical action of separatio "may be wrongly applied, in which case it will be destructive. It is improper to divide an organic whole mechanically in the name of an arbitrary notion of equality." Paris tried to evade his responsibility by suggesting that the apple be divided into three equal parts, but this was not allowed. Edinger then relates another story of the judgment of Solomon, in which two women come before Solomon, each claiming to be the mother of the same child:

Bring me a sword said the king; and a sword was brought into the King's presence. "Cut the living child in two," the King said, "and give half to one, half to the other." At this the woman who was the mother of the living child addressed the king, for she burned with pity for her son. "If it please you, my lord," she said, "let them give her the child; only do not let them think of killing it!" But the other said, "He shall belong to neither of us. Cut him up." Then the king gave his decision. "Give the child to the first woman," he said, "and do not kill him. She is his mother." All Israel came to hear of the judgment the king had pronounced, and held the king in awe, recognizing that he possessed divine wisdom for dispending justice. (1 Kings 3:24-28, JB, as cited in Edinger, 1985, p. 194 - 195)

Psychologically speaking, there would come about a very destructive separation of the twenty-nine allied nations if the main accord between them, the NATO alliance, was dissolved. It would lead to a major separation between and among all the member states. In addition, this separation would then allow Putin to further divide and conquer, which could include conventional warfare to gain back Russian satellite countries of the former USSR, thereby crossing further "red lines" that NATO would have reacted too; but also, cyber and psychological warfare, which, as in the case of Germany and its population, appear to be generally brainwashed by Putin and Russia. It is a scary spectacle. But it is real and it is with us now.

The only thing preventing Putin from conventionally invading independent countries such as the Baltic States (Estonia, Latvia, and Lithuania) right now is the potential threat to him that NATO still poses, at least for now. It is his greatest wish that it dissolves, and it makes one question why Donald Trump is supportive of that position. NATO must stay strong now in the face of this adversity. Indeed, it is just for moments such as today historically that it was created to begin with. It cannot be allowed to be dismembered. The alternative is unspeakable.

CHAPTER SIX

Mortificatio: France and the
Death of Culture

The true history of the mind is not preserved in learned volumes but in the living psychic organism of every individual.

— C. G. JUNG (1954)

E dinger (1985, p. 148) tells us that mortificatio "is the most negative operation in alchemy. It has to do with darkness, defeat, torture, mutilation, death, and rotting. However, these dark images often lead to highly positive ones—growth, resurrection, and rebirth—but the hallmark of mortification is the color black." In the Lives of the Alchemical Philosophers it states: "That which does not make black cannot make white, because blackness is the beginning of whiteness, and a sign of putrefaction and alteration, and that body is now penetrated and mortified." (as cited in Edinger, p. 148–149)

Psychologically speaking, blackness refers to the shadow, which is the term Jung used to refer to the part of the unconscious that holds all of our rejected and disowned traits and actions. To become aware of the shadow is to bring whiteness to the blackness, as is bringing light or consciousness to something that had been unconscious; in the shadows, so to speak.

The shadow of the country of France presently is the fact that as a rising immigration of Muslim populations flooded into the country, many from former French colonies in North Africa, the Jewish population is moving out of France in droves. France contains both the largest Jewish population and the largest Muslim population in all of Europe. The fact of the matter is that anti-Semitism is a greater problem in France than anywhere else on the continent. Kirchick (2017) reports:

> *In a speech to the National Assembly after the terrorist attacks of January, 2015, which took the lives of seventeen people, French Prime Minister Manuel Valls, the son of Spanish immigrants, declared: "If 100,000 French people of Spanish origin were to leave, I would never say that France is not France anymore. But if 100,000 French Jews leave, France will no longer be France. The French Republic will be a failure. (p.136)*

Apparently, the speech did not prevent 8,000 French Jews from moving to Israel in the following year, part of the largest migration of Western European Jews to Israel since it was founded in 1948.

The killings from the terrorist attacks of January 2015 included four Jews who were killed by a terrorist at the Hyper Cacher kosher supermarket, after nineteen people had been taken hostage, and fourteen people murdered at the offices of the satirical weekly magazine Charlie Hebdo, which had published a humorous depiction of Mohammed on a recent front cover. The gunmen, brothers Said and Cherif Kouachi, apparently were not amused, and this was their revenge. The brothers identified themselves as belonging to the Islamist terrorist group Al-Qaida, in the Arabian Peninsula, which took responsibility for the attack.

While there was an outpouring of grief and support for both the Hyper Cacher and Charlie Hebdo victims in the aftermath, there is still a deeper problem for the Jews. This is because Western European Jews are often criticized for the behavior of the state of Israel, over which they have no control. As Kirchick (2017) states: "When you combine this guilt by association with the view, embraced by 59 percent of Europeans, that Israel is the greatest threat to world peace, then European Jews become implicated for every sin, real or imagined, committed by that much loathed state"(p. 137).

Psychologically speaking, this lack of differentiation—consider the alchemical operation of separatio in this instance—that projects the responsibility and guilt of Israel's actions onto the Jewish citizens of Western Europe is both primitive and dangerous. It is just such lazy reasoning that underlies so much discrimination of any group. This type of thinking needs to "grow up" and become more adult-like. The peace of the world in the future depends on this. To continue with the same sloppy primitive mode of thinking, shockingly shared by a majority of Europeans, is neither acceptable nor tolerable. If this situation is not thought through to a more logical position, more explosive problems in the future will ensue—for both Jews and non-Jews. Kirchick (2017) continues:

> For Europeans, Jews are not just fellow citizens: they are also painful living reminders of their nations' and ancestors' historic criminality, the remnant of the people an earlier generation of Europeans tried to murderously expunge from the human race. Responses to the social trauma engendered by this memory generally take three forms. A plurality of Europeans are apathetic, wholly ignorant of Jews on an individual or historical level, but vaguely aware that something bad happened to them many years ago. A conscientious minority commit themselves to dutiful commemoration of the Holocaust as a unique and unprecedented evil, to preservation and enrichment of contemporary Jewish life, and to political affinity with Israel as the democratic homeland of the Jewish people. Another minority, more prevalent today on the left than on the right, engage in overwrought and highly disproportionate condemnation of Israel, sometimes via comparison to the

Third Reich, rendering Jews the new Nazis. In this reduc-
tionist reading, European Jews are an extension of the
Israeli state, and crude anti-Semitism, when expressed by
Muslims or their sympathizers, is for the most part an ill-
mannered venting of an otherwise legitimate anti-imperi-
alism. (p. 139)

I would argue that it is just this sort of primitive thinking that must undergo a transformation, so as to ensure that the death of culture within France does not take place, as it most certainly is at the moment. This primitive thinking is the essence of the dark shadow that now hovers over France, owing to this extraordinary conflation that France's Jewish citizens are responsible for the actions of the state of Israel. The fact is that the Jewish citizens of France are the victims of a negative projection from a majority of the French and European population.

This dark shadow or blackness represents the prima materia that must be transformed through light and consciousness. Symbolically, something must be sacrificed, and commonly it takes the form of the dragon that must be slayed by the hero. Jung tells us: "The slaying of the dragon is the mortificatio of the first, dangerous, poisonous stage of the Anima/Mercurious, freed from her imprisonment in the prima materia."

The dragon is the personification of the instinctual psyche and a synonym for the prima materia. In one alchemical text the slaying of the king, representing the old ruling principle or dominant cultural consciousness, is equated with the slaying of the dragon:

I am an infirm and weak old man, surnamed the dragon;
therefore am I shut up in a cave, that I may be ransomed
by the kingly crown...A fiery sword inflicts great torments
upon me; death makes weak my flesh and bones...My soul
and my spirit depart; a terrible poison, I am likened to the
black raven, for that is the wages of sin; in dust and earth I
lie, that out of three may come One. O soul and spirit, leave

*me not, that I may see again the light of day, and the hero
of peace whom the whole world shall behold may arise from
me. (Jung, 1954, par. 733)*

Edinger (1985, p.152) explains: "The infirm and weak old man represents a conscious dominant or spiritual principle that has lost its effectiveness. It has regressed to the level of the primordial psyche (dragon) and therefore must submit to transformation." In essence, it is only by bringing more consciousness into the present situation that the dark instinctual psychic energy, which now threatens the entire continent of Europe, can be transformed. The regressive view of anti-Semitism, along with a paranoia of immigration, which is shared by the majority of Europeans, including the French, will only serve to strengthen the hand of the supporters of ultra-right political parties, which, by and large, support illiberal democracies. France, too, shares this problem.

Marine Le Pen and the Front National

The term Islamophobia came into existence based upon a 1997 report by the Runnemede Trust, a UK think-tank. The study criticized groups that it thought to be prejudiced against Islam —that is, groups that were not willing to debate Islamist ideas and practices as being equal to Western ideas and practices. As Kirchick (2017, p. 149) states: "The report thus insidiously conflated legitimate concerns about Islamist practices and political aims with far more questionable positions; It became impermissible—Islamophobic—to refuse to 'debate,' never mind refute, even the most rancid Islamist conspiracy theories or to report factually on intolerance or the stifling of dissent within Muslim communities."

Kirchick (2017, p.149) further points out that the use of the word phobic itself is fraught with danger, as it is a word borrowed from psychoanalysis referring to an "'irrational fear of a non-existent threat.' 'Islamophobia' thus undermines statements of the

obvious: Namely, that there is a demonstrable connection between Islamist ideologies and terrorism." This further lack of
separatio or psychological differentiation regarding the actual
threat of certain Islamist beliefs with terrorism defies common
sense. It also creates an atmosphere of fear that Marine Le Pen
and her Front National party are now capitalizing on, as the main
French Nationalist Populist Party.

As in Germany and the United Kingdom, the main center-right
and center-left political parties in France do not allow any criticism of Islam. To criticize Islam is to both be racist and "Islamophobic." This is simply not tolerated. And so you have former
center-right and center-left voters leaving their traditional parties in large numbers, inflating the ranks of various nationalist
populist parties that are only too happy to bring these disen-
chanted voters into their fold. No matter that these new voters
are getting much more than they bargained for with their new
radical right-wing parties.

In France with Marine Le Pen and the Nationalist Front, the
situation is particularly bad. As Kirchick (2017, p. 150) reports:

> Her [Le Pen's] National Front is the leading political party
> among workers, farmers, youth, and the unemployed.
> Though always categorized as "far right," the National
> Front is pulling away many traditional Socialist voters.
> So extensive is its support that it is frankly inaccurate to
> call the party "far" anything: It can claim to represent as
> broad a cross-section of the French public as the ruling So-
> cialists or conservative Gaullists. Le Pen's foreign policy is
> anti-European, anti-American, and pro-Russian; in 2014,
> her party received a loan of 11 million pounds sterling
> from a Russian bank, and two years later she publically
> requested 27 million more pounds to fight in the presiden-
> tial election.... A Le Pen administration would only prolong
> France's economic misery, if not hasten a further decline.
> Were she ever to be elected president, it would be a disaster

for European unity, trans-atlanticism, and the assertion of
liberal values abroad.

More than anything it is Le Pen's ongoing attacks against Islam as an undermining force in France that bolster her attraction to disenfranchised voters from other parties and swell her ranks. But there is also no doubt that, as with other countries and leaders, it is pure opportunism on Le Pen's part, with a willingness to exploit the fear of the electorate of an invasion of Islamists into their countries. In other words, the objective problem is not nearly as bad as Le Pen is scripting it to be, but the narrative of fear of invasion from the "other" is a very effective rallying cry —as Putin, Trump, and Orban have conclusively shown in Russia, the United States, and Hungary.

Attempts have been made to repress the racism and anti-Semitism within the party's philosophy, to make it a more attractive party, even for Jews. But as Kirchick (2017) reports: "Reputable polling shows the party's rank and file continue to harbor anti-Semitic views; 48 percent, for instance, believe 'Jews have too much power in the media.' Nonetheless, it is to this political faction that so many of France's disillusioned voters are rallying. A feeling that political elites are ignoring or even abetting the slow erosion of the Republic's secular nature feeds Marine Le Pens rise" (p.151).

In the summer of 2013 my wife Kate and I traveled to a rural part of France—a southern section of the Massif Central—to walk through the gorgeous countryside of the thinly populated Aubrac region. This is part of the famed pilgrimage "Camino de Santiago de Compostela" that begins in Le Puy en Velay in France and continues all the way to Galicia in northwestern Spain. It was a spectacular 200 kilometers through forests, countryside, and ancient medieval towns, such as St. Chely de Aubrac, Estaing, and Conques—all UNESCO world heritage sites that parallel the old Roman road between Lyons and Toulouse.

The region is famous for its bovine breeding, which is the

main activity on the plateau, literally named the "Aubrac," a species that is well adapted to the sparse environment. The cows are bred for their meat, whereas before the 1960s, they were bred for their dairy products. The milk was made into cheese in burons or mazucs, which are small structures in the middle of the pastures. Today, the majority of these structures are in ruin. The "Laguiole" (pronounced Layole) cheese is now only made by a dairy in the village of Laguiole, which is also famous for its knives.

On our first night in the region, we stayed in a farmhouse with a farm couple and several other guests, all from other parts of France. It is easy to see from this perspective that these rural folk, who are not unsophisticated, would be of the opinion that they would like their lives to stay as much as possible as they are, unfettered by globalism and mass immigration from other countries. Traditions here go back hundreds of years, and there exists a natural conservatism that comes with this in their collective cultural psyche. They understand that times are changing, and they have done their best to adapt to the changes, but the pace of change is what most concerns them, and rightly so. Their needs have to be taken into account by politicians, and they will support those people who best understand their needs and promise to address them.

If these individuals all feel that their needs are being ignored by the center-right and center-left parties, it is to be expected that they would gravitate to the message of Marine Le Pen, who is listening to them, whereas the other parties are not. And in the process, they may just turn a blind eye to some of the more extreme views within the party. As we know, this blind-eye phenomenon is just what happened in the 2016 American election, which helped to elect Donald Trump, an outsider who, though brash and insulting, did not represent the status quo. Many voters, especially those in the rural heartland and industrial rust-belt of the United States, felt that Trump was seeing them in a way the more establishment candidates, such as Hillary Clinton, were not.

Once again, now in France, we see the old order of rule dying. As in Britain, Germany, and the United States, the center-right and center-left parties that have been governing for the past 75 years, since the end of World War II, are now in complete disarray. They're elitism, political correctness, and sense of entitlement overcame them. This is especially true in the three decades since the fall of the Berlin Wall. And now they find themselves becoming increasingly irrelevant to a huge sector of their own populations. The disparity between the wealthy elites—the top one percent in these societies—and the rest of the population has grown exponentially over this time, and is no doubt fueling the flames of unrest.

In the meantime, it is the nationalist populist parties in all of these countries that are growing, and in some places, soaring, in popularity. Psychologically speaking, it is important to understand that there does need to be a mortificatio of the old ruling principle of the now elite center-right and center-left parties. But replacing them with nationalist populist parties that tout fear, anger, racism, anti-Semitism, and anti-immigration—that would endanger NATO and the European Union, and invite Russia in as equal member of the world order—would have devastating effects on world stability and the balance of power.

In psychological terms, what must die, must die, but it also must be replaced by something superior and more advanced, rather than inferior and regressive. It must be something that appeals to the better angels of our nature, rather than our inner demons.

CHAPTER SEVEN

Coagulatio: Hungary and the Fixation of Viktor Orban

> *In essence, coagulatio is the process that turns something into earth. "Earth" is thus one of the synonyms for the coagulatio. It is heavy and permanent, of fixed position and shape. It doesn't disappear into the air by volatizing nor pliantly adapt itself to the shape of any container as does water. Its form and location are fixed. Thus, for a psychic content to become earth means that it has become concretized in a particular localized form; that is, it has become attached to an ego.*
>
> — EDINGER (1985 P. 83)

Just as calcinatio is the operation of the element fire and solutio the operation of the element of water, so coagulatio represents the operation of the element of the earth. In this alchemical and psychological sense, the politics of Hungary have become concretized in a particular localized form in the ego of their leader, Viktor Orban. First elected in 2010, he has worked steadily to replace Hungary's multi-party democracy with a one party "illiberal democracy," patterned after the models of government in Russia under Putin and Turkey under Erdogan. Madeline Albright (2018) explains:

> *An illiberal democracy is centered on the supposed needs of the community rather than the inalienable rights of the individual. It is democratic because it respects the will of the majority; illiberal because it disregards the concerns of*

the minority.... This thinking is illiberal, and an echo of
the jingoistic nationalism that carried Mussolini to power
a century ago. (p. 172)

Historically an anti-Communist and a liberal who attended
Oxford University on a scholarship from a foundation owned
by Hungarian-born billionaire George Soros (who Orban now demonizes as an enemy of the state), Orban has proven to be very
flexible in his political philosophy, depending on the time and
place. In his present incarnation, Orban has calculated that he can
justify the dismantling of the Hungarian democracy to suit his
own needs of wanting to stay in power indefinitely like his men-
tors, Putin and Erdogan. And like them, he is capitalizing on the
fears of his electorate, in particular the fear of the nation being inundated by Muslim immigrants from the Middle East—this, despite the fact that very few immigrants ever settle in Hungary.
But the very fear of it can be weaponized politically in national
populist rhetoric, as we have witnessed in the Unites States with
Trump and his obsession with building a wall along our southern
border with Mexico. In reality, there are many more Canadians
from the northern border who overstay their visas in the United
States. As Albright (2018, p. 184) writes regarding immigration in
Hungary:

Instead of working constructively with regional and global
institutions to stabilize the flow of migrants and meet hu-
manitarian needs, Orban has chosen to foment paranoia.
Ignoring the fact that relatively few migrants are clamoring
to enter Hungary, the prime minister declared: "The masses
arriving from other civilizations endanger our way of life,
our culture, our customs, and our Christian traditions." He
said migrants would bring "crime and terror ... mass dis-
order... riots ... [and] gangs hunting down our women and
daughters."

Orban is selling his perception of reality to the Hungarian electorate, based upon fear mongering and a disregard of the objective facts on the ground—a hallmark of tyranny historically. Unfortunately, Orban's tainted message is coagulating very well with a majority of Hungarians.

In the process, Orban is revising Hungarian history by making the country out to be the victims of a Nazi "invasion" during the Second World War, despite the fact that the Germans were welcomed into the country on condition that Hungary regain the two-thirds of its greater territory that was lost after being allied with Germany and Austria in the First World War. Orban has memorialized this by creating a "Day of National Cohesion," on June 4 of each year, which commemorates the signing of the Treaty of Trianon, complaining about "the unjust and unfair dismemberment of the Hungarian nation by foreign powers" (Kirchick, 2017, p. 47). Kirchick continues:

> *Ignoring the reasons why Hungary lost two-thirds of its territory—namely, its membership in the belligerent axes of both World Wars—this annual day of mourning calls on Hungarians to wallow in victimhood and nurture feelings of resentment toward the Allied victors.... Hungarian government statements, museums, memorials, and other instruments of its history policy seem intended to create the perception that Hungary was a victim of the conflict, rather than one of its perpetrators. (p. 47-48)*

The reality of the German occupation of Hungary during the Second World War is that over 500,000 Jews were rounded up and sent off to their deaths at Auschwitz by Hungarian police and citizenry, with very little oversight by their German "occupiers." This happened while under the leadership of Hungarian authoritarian leader Miklos Horthy, who had passed the first anti-Semitic law of Hungary in 1920. As Kirchick reports (2017), "So able and willing were the Nazi's Hungarian accomplices that Adolph Eichmann, the SS officer in charge of deporting the Jews to the death camps, managed to oversee the gruesome task with just 200 Germans at his command."(p.41)

This revisionist history from Orban has been girded by a revisionist piece of community sculpture entitled Monument to the Victims of German Occupation. The sculpture, completed in 2014, depicts an innocent nation, Hungary, represented by the archangel Michael, being attacked by the Nazi eagle from above. Thus it is surmised that all Hungarians suffered under the occupation of the Germans, not just Jews. The fact that the Jews were persecuted by their own countrymen and that 500,000 were summarily shipped off to Auschwitz and exterminated, after being rounded up by their own countrymen, is completely whitewashed. As is the fact that if Germany had prevailed in World War II, Hungary would have made good on the bet to have invited Germany into their territory at the beginning of the conflict, and presumably been given back the two-thirds of their territory which was lost after World War I in the Treaty of Trianon. Kirchick (2017) makes the point that "by obscuring Jewish victimhood entirely and ascribing total innocence to Hungarians and total evil to Germans, the memorial is as factually deceptive and politically exploitative as any Stalinist icon" (p.43)

A more appropriate and historically accurate memorial to the persecuted Jews in Hungary during World War II can be found on the shores of the Danube River in Budapest, within a stone's throw of the Hungarian Parliament buildings. It is called "Shoes on the Danube Bank," and marks the last standing place of Jews who were told to take off their shoes before being shot and thrown into the fast flowing river below. This happened, mind you, each and every day during the war.

This atrocity was carried out by the so-called Arrow Cross militiamen, the Hungarian accomplices of the Nazis. It is both jarring and repugnant to the soul to stand on this spot and take in the sixty pairs of bronzed shoes and wonder about the fates of these innocent victims of a mass psychosis that had spread from Berlin to Budapest. Just a small representation of the total of 75 million lives lost during this time as the result of one psychopathic madman, Hitler, and his influence spreading and engendering his psychosis in millions of others.

The coagulation of this victim mentality that Orban engenders within the psyche of his fellow citizens through the manipulation of their emotions is no less hideous—in spirit if not in scope—than what Hitler was up to 90 years ago in 1930s Germany. And as the Hungarian people have, for the most part, bought into this manipulation, Orban has taken the opportunity to begin to dismantle the democracy he was elected to defend. As Albright (2018) points out regarding Orban: "He is a thin skinned opportunist who likes to command. It would be an exaggeration to suggest that he has forced Hungary into a Fascist straightjacket, but he is encouraging his country to feel comfortable in a loose-fitting ultranationalist jacket"(p.173). Albright (2018) continues:

> Since 2010, Fidesz has used its executive and legislative clout to rewrite the constitution in a way that expands the powers of the prime minister while diminishing those of parliament. To widen the circle of conservative votes, the government extended citizenship privileges to ethnic Hungarians living outside the country. Party loyalists have taken control of the constitutional court, the National Elections Commission, and much of the judiciary. The administration has replaced public radio and television channels with state operated media, sapped the strength of labor unions, reshaped educational curricula, and attempted to dictate the content of movies and plays. Coziness between public ministries and a new generation of oligarchs has given Fidesz a rich source of financial backing—and abundant opportunities for corruption. (p.173)

Orban goes about his work with panache, criticizing the European Union, of which his country was admitted into in 2005, and promises his countrymen that he will liberate them now from Brussels and its over-reaching laws that affect the daily lives of Hungarian citizens. This is despite the fact that Hungary receives many more dollars from the EU than it contributes, and benefits greatly economically from being an EU member. But in order to justify increasingly undemocratic measures at home, one must identify enemies abroad, and the European Union serves this purpose now for Orban.

More than this, Orban is now seen as a leader of right-wing nationalist populist movements all across Europe, not just in his home country. And so, the likes of Nigel Farage of the UK Independence Party in Britain and Marine Le Pen of the Front National in France revere him; and Vladimir Putin has praised him for "re-thinking history," as indeed Putin has done with regard to Stalinist times in the old Soviet Union.

One Hungarian film that may have escaped the notice of state censors (because it is told in an allegorical fashion) is a film entitled White God. The film follows the life of a mixed-breed dog, Hagen, who lives with 13-year-old Lili and her divorced father. The father wants to get rid of Hagen because having a "mutt" means you have to pay a special tax to the state. The father promises to get Lili a pure-breed dog instead. But Lili loves Hagen and totally resists the idea of giving him up.

After the father dumps Hagen out on the side of a highway, Lili and her father become estranged, and Hagen begins a dark journey through several owners until he ends up being rounded up and sent to a dog pound. Facing imminent death, Hagen breaks out of the dog pound and releases all of the other dogs. They form a ferocious army of "mutts" who begin rampaging the city. At the door of the slaughterhouse where Lili's father works, just as the dogs are ready to tear him apart, Lili confronts Hagen, who is now leader of the pack. She begins to play Franz Liszt's Hungarian Rhapsody No. 2 on her trumpet. Hagen lies down to listen and all of the other dogs lie down in unison, signifying a resolution of the conflict.

It is a powerful metaphor of how immigrants are being treated by the government and the majority of citizens in Hungary, and points towards the higher cultural achievements of the nation as represented by Franz Listz, it's most famous composer, and his Hungarian Rhapsody No. 2. The transcendence of Listz's cultural achievement is set out as an antidote to the narrow-mindedness and fear-mongering of the present times. As Albright (2018) writes:

> The whole notion of pure blood is laughable, but that does not stop tribal instincts and their accompanying national mythologies from exercising a powerful sway over behavior, as World War II tragically demonstrated. It took the shock of that war to create a reaction strong enough for countries to embrace regional integration, but that choice was always more compelling logically than emotionally. (p. 178)

Perhaps this is the problem facing the European Union today: that even though it is pragmatically a successful idea and prevents nationalist populist ideas from taking root, for the most part, it lacks emotional gravitas. It is based more upon economics than on any deeply rooted spiritual principle. And on an emotional level it simply cannot compete with nationalist populism, the old tribalism that seems to refuse to die at any cost. And it is this soft underbelly of democracy that is exploited in such a predatorily way by feral-like politicians such as Orban, Putin, and Trump.

These "leaders" know precisely how to get an emotional rise out of their populations, and they will never hesitate to seize an opportunity to do so. While their political opponents may make an argument based upon facts and logic, these simply don't seem to matter to them or indeed many of their supporters. This problem also underlines the fact that so many people in today's world are treacherously ignorant of many facts, and worse, do not care. In fact, many are more likely to support conspiracy theories than real facts. The psychological immaturity of the populations of these countries allows these predatory leaders to exploit them repeatedly, even when the policies they enact enrich others at their own expense, and their governments are filled with corruption.

One key factor for all of these countries is the fear of being overwhelmed by immigrants from foreign countries. This is a legitimate concern that must be faced honestly in a balanced way by their governments. The solution is not to have an open-door policy, nor to be completely closed to it. Strong and effective policies for legal immigration must be put in place, with an awareness of what is causing the problem to begin with. As Madeline Albright (2018), herself an immigrant to the United States from Czechoslovakia after World War II, states: "In general, the movement of people from their homes—the leaving behind of possessions, familiar sights, memories, and ancestral graveyards—does not occur without good cause. Most of us would prefer to remain in places where our names are known, our customs accepted, and our languages spoken." (p. 186)

To simply vilify groups of people from specific countries as evil and to misuse or abuse the opportunity of refugees escaping their homelands out of a shear necessity for survival are simply wrong and immoral. This treatment of the "other" reflects the evil that is being projected onto immigrants and refugees psychologically from the shadow of the dominant group. Edinger (1985, p. 91) tells us this:

> In fact, coagulation is explicitly associated with evil. This is demonstrated by the alchemical connection of coagulation with Saturn, the malefic principle (i.e. Saturn is known to possess the attributes of vileness, evil, rottenness, and oppressiveness). One text says; 'the coagulation takes place

in Saturn.' According to Jacob Boheme, 'Saturn, that cold, sharp, austere and astringent regent, taketh its beginning and original not from the sun; for Saturn hath in its power the chamber of death, and is a drier up of powers, from whence corporeity existeth. For as the Sun is the heart of life, and an original of all spirits in the body of the world, so Saturn is a beginner of all corporeity and comprehensibility or palpability.'

Orban epitomizes the incarnation of evil with his dark and old machinations to convince the Hungarian people that they are long-suffering victims of history whose vindication is now at hand under the protection of their new strong-man, namely, himself. And the whole world is against them and so he must further protect them by dismantling the democracy in which he was elected, to run a more focused and stronger illiberal democracy, which he will head going into the unknown future.

Unfortunately, his inflated and entitled ego discounts the dark lessons of history, of which all Hungarians and all Europeans should be very well aware: namely, that well over one hundred million people were slaughtered through two world wars just in the past century. And inevitably it was at the hands of those governments and leaders who could not resist the temptation of asserting their power by reinforcing their own tribalism and nationalism and a demonization of anyone "other." Their quest, from Kaiser Wilhelm to Mussolini, Hirohito, and Hitler, was to rule the world; a world that only ended up in ruin—as it will surely again, if the likes of Orban, Putin, and Trump get a hold on enough power through their evil incantations to their populations; those unconscious souls who are far too primitive psychologically not to take the populist bait that their leaders shovel into them.

Salvation can come only through a maturation of these populations' psychology, one person at a time. The fear is that if enough individuals do not confront their own dark shadow within themselves, they will continue to project it onto the "other." And if we do not assimilate the devil within our own souls, then the devil will undoubtedly devour us. Presently that devil and that evil are manifesting in the likes of Viktor Orban, and the prognosis for Hungary and Europe is unfortunately not favorable. What is required now, and is likely the only antidote for the likes of Orban, would be for Europeans to coagulate a deeper spiritual connection within the European Union based upon shared values and the principles of democracy — equality, individuality, and truth — and not merely as an economic union.

CHAPTER EIGHT

Sublimatio: Surveying the
New Sultan of Turkey

The archetype – let us never forget this – is a psychic organ present in all of us. A bad explanation means a correspondingly bad attitude to this organ, which may thus be injured. But the ultimate sufferer is the bad interpreter himself.

— C. G. JUNG (1954)

J ust as the operation of calcinatio pertains to fire, solutio to water, and coagulatio to earth, so sublimatio pertains to the operation of air (Edinger, 1985, p. 117). More specifically, it is the operation that allows us to get above a concrete situation and perceive it from above, just as a hot air balloon can float suspended above the earth, providing a fine view of an extended landscape. In a similar fashion we can look down upon developments over the past twenty years in the country of Turkey and see where their increasingly authoritarian leader, Recep Tayyip Erdogan, has taken them.

In order to understand the present trajectory of Turkey and its ruling regime, we must go back to Erdogan's upbringing (born in 1954) in a poor part of Istanbul, where he grew up in the 1960s and 1970s with religious Muslim parents who had immigrated to the city from the impoverished northeastern province of Rize on the Black Sea. Soner Cagaptay writes in his 2017 book The New Sultan: Erdogan and the Crises of Modern Turkey: "The experience of growing up in this rough-hewn, conservative area, the 'bad zip code' part of Istanbul, would forever shape his view of the 'other,' that is, Turkey's elite rich, westernized communities and their secularist, Kemalist ideology. Even when Erdogan entered business in the 1990s and became wealthy, he maintained his contempt for this elite." (p. 16)

The new nation of Turkey arose out of the remains of the Ottoman Empire, which had ruled in the area for hundreds of years prior to its collapse after World War I. The new nation was ruled by the father of modern Turkey, Mustafa Kemal Ataturk. Kemal was a former officer in the Ottoman army who ruled from 1923 until 1938 as president. He was pro-European and a secularist who abolished the caliphate and demoted Islam from being the official religion of the state. He initiated governmental reforms, including a civil code from Switzerland, criminal laws from Italy, and a centralized and nationalist model of territorial administration from France. (Cagaptay, 2017, pp. 20–21)

Conversely, Erdogan was encouraged by his father to enroll in religious schools, which he embraced and thrived within, despite the dominant secularist Kemalist philosophy of the times. Religious studies had been relegated, for the most part, to the private sector.

In 1950, four years before Erdogan was born, Turkey held its first democratic elections. In that election, the Republican People's Party (CHP), Ataturk's legacy, was routed by the Democratic Party (DP). The CHP today is the only formidable opposition to the Justice and Development Party (AKP), Erdogan's governing party. Erdogan rose within the political ranks by first becoming mayor of Istanbul from 1994 to 1998. He created the AKP in 2001 from the remnants of the former Welfare Party (WP).

Since 2001, Erdogan and his party have now won six separate elections, including three parliamentary elections, one presidential election, and two national referenda. And his hold on power has increased exponentially during that time due to his systematic silencing of all of his detractors. However, the country remains deeply divided over his leadership and his policies. Cagaptay (2017) writes:

The country is polarized between supporters and opponents of Erdogan, who has won successive elections since 2002 on a platform of right-wing populism. He is the archetype of the anti-elitist, nationalist, and conservative politicians on the rise around the world. He has demonized and cracked down on electoral constituencies that are not likely to vote for him, a strategy that has dramatically worsened the polarization in Turkey, which is now sharply split between pro and anti-Erdogan camps; the former, a conservative and Turkish nationalist right-wing coalition, believes that the country is paradise; the latter, a loose group of leftists, secularists, liberals, and Kurds, thinks that it lives in hell ... in short Turkey is in crisis. (pp. 1–2)

Turkey is a key state within the Middle East, acting as a buffer and a balance between several large players, including Iran, Syria, and Israel. So Turkey's stability within is critical to the stability of the surrounding region, which is already fraught with problems that affect all of us on a global level. And the best Turkey would be a Turkey that is a healthy democracy. Instead Erdogan has taken the country in the opposite direction.

Erdogan, like all nationalist populists, always claims he has the best interests of the common people as his guidepost. And that may sound true from his rhetoric. But by championing the will of only the majority of people, he is, de facto, attacking the country's minorities and their rights. And this, of course, has consequences.

On the night of July 16, 2016, there was a coup attempt against Erdogan, during which he barely escaped an assassination squad descending on his vacation villa, while the Turkish Air Force bombed the capital city, Ankara—the first time the city had been attacked since the 15th century. Although the coup attempt was soon cut short, it sent shock waves throughout the country and around the world. Blame was placed at the feet of the

Gulenists, followers of Fatallah Gulen and his religious and educational movement that had possessed enormous informal political power for decades in Turkey and was largely responsible for the political rise of Erdogan in politics. Around 2011, Erdogan began to think that he no longer needed the Gulenists support any longer—but only after he had used the Gulenists to subdue the power of the TAF (Turkish Armed Forces) first, which had resulted in thousands of military officers being displaced, with many also being arrested.

The political agility that Erdogan has demonstrated in eliminating his opposition, one player at a time, playing opposing forces off against each other, is frankly impressive and purely Machiavellian. Erdogan's rise to power has also been greatly aided by a booming economy in the first decade of the twenty-first century. Cagaptay (2017) states:

> When Erdogan's AKP came to power in 2002, Turkey was a country of mostly poor people; it is now mostly a country of middle-income citizens. Life has improved, and citizens enjoy better infrastructure and services overall. In 2002, Turkey's maternal-mortality rate was roughly comparable to prewar Syria's; now it is close to Spain's. In other words Turks used to live like citizens of Syria, but now they live like Spaniards. That is why Erdogan remains wildly popular and wins elections, even though Turkey's per capita income has inched up only incrementally since the "miracle" surge between 2002 and 2008. (p. 5)

The future success of Erdogan staying in power will likely be tied to Turkey's economic performance, which is diminishing presently. Their economy would also be greatly affected by any global recession, which is where we seem to be headed in the latter half of 2019. In spite of that happening, Erdogan has already established himself as one of the historically great leaders of Turkey, not unlike Mustafa Kemal Ataturk. Both wanted to restore

Turkey to greatness again, as in the glory days of the Ottoman Empire. The Ottoman Empire controlled much of Southwest Europe, Western Asia, Eastern Europe, and the Caucasus and North Africa between the early 14th and 20th centuries. Its zenith occurred under Suleiman the Magnificent, who ruled the empire from 1520 to 1566.

The contrast is that Mustafa Kemal Ataturk wanted to ensure the former empire's greatness by having a secular government that was not beholding to the Muslim religion—a separation of church and state, as was the case in all of the Western democracies of the last century in Europe and the Americas. This was a very radical departure from the past for Kemal, but for the most part it was successful in that it led Turkey into a prosperous and democratic future.

Recip Tayyip Erdogan wants to make Turkey great again by reversing all of what Kemal had accomplished over his 15-year rule, and by those who followed him. In doing so, Erdogan has polarized his country and led it into an almost unresolvable crisis, which could implode at any time.

Psychologically speaking, what Erdogan has accomplished is to successfully lead the country into an abyss of regression, similar to what Trump has done in the United States in the last three years and what Orban has accomplished in Hungary over the last decade. All of them have relied on Vladimir Putin's playbook in how to dismantle a democracy, one step at a time. First, democratic institutions within the country are attacked, beginning with the media as "an enemy of the people"; then the judicial wing is brought under the stringent influence of the executive; and third, a one-party system is created by eliminating free and fair elections. Ultimately, only a tyrannical leader is left in place who is inflated psychologically and a danger to everyone around him or her, especially the minorities in the country, whom the leader demonizes constantly in order to solidify the base.

Edinger (1985, p. 123) tells us that sublimatio can also mean "grinding" or "hammering" to bring about an attenuation of material (i.e., a thinning of a thick material).

Very fine powder approaches a gas in its consistency. Note also that the symbolism of grinding contains the moral categories of good and bad. Powder made up of small particles is called "fine". That with large particles is "coarse." To be good is to be well pulverized. Encounter with the numinosium may have a pulverizing effect, as indicated by the saying, "Though the mills of God may grind slowly, they grind exceedingly small." "Foliation" has the same implication. One (alchemical) recipe reads. "Sow your gold in white foliated earth" — that is, in sublimated earth. Foliation is done by hammering.

There is a definite "coarseness" to Erdogan's illiberal democracy, as indeed there is with all illiberal democracies. And it is not a "fine" thing that he is alienating half the population of Turkey on any given day. The simple interpretation of democracy as a "majority" rule is not sufficient because it then "enslaves" anyone in the democracy who is part of the minority.

For malignant narcissists such as Putin, Trump, Orban, and now Erdogan, it could be said that they run their countries on the central motto of "divide and conquer." But unbeknownst to them, this strategy represses the more historically significant theme that "a divided house cannot stand." This is the hammer that in the fullness of time will pulverize the coarseness of these regimes, built on hate, fear, and a projection of the shadow onto the "other".

One of the most transparently "coarse" events for the country almost a decade ago occurred when Erdogan, in 2010, sponsored a referendum for 26 proposed amendments to the constitution, the purpose of which was ostensibly to create a constitution that was more in line with European Union member states, thus facilitating the process of joining the EU. Opposition to the referendum was significant, and many warned that more liberal provisions of the referendum would likely never be implemented (such as gender reform and gay rights), and further that the door was being opened for Erdogan to seize control of the courts by increasing the number of members who sit on them.

The government manipulated the voting process so that there was to be a single "Yes" or "No" for all 26 amendments, ultimately making it a referendum on the Erdogan government itself. Erdogan won the vote by a 58–42% margin and never did implement any of the liberal reforms he promised he would. He did, however, take over control of the courts by stacking them with his supporters by increasing the number of seats on the Supreme Court and lower courts in Turkey, thus subsuming the judicial branch of government under his control.

Erdogan followed up this indignity to the democracy in the election of 2011, where he was heavily favored to win a third term in office as prime minister. He did achieve a 49.8% of the vote, and in the process solidified his tyrannical hold on power. Cagaptay writes (2017, p. 127):

> With Erdogan and his party in charge of the executive, legislative and judicial branches, a comprehensive and thorough crackdown on opposition media taking place, a significant part of the public aligned with him, and perhaps most importantly, the TAF (Turkish Armed Forces) in a severely weakened state, Erdogan's illiberal alter ego encountered even fewer constraints after 2011.

The pattern of Erdogan in power, beginning with his initial distaste for the secular wealthy and the powerful within Turkish society, has been to gain increasing personal power for himself at the expense of the secular elite, and to consolidate this power through illiberal reforms at a steady pace, whenever the opportunity presents itself. But the former secular elite in Turkey still control much of the country's wealth, and it is unlikely Erdogan will ever be able to subdue them completely. In the meantime they, along with all the other minorities in Turkey, wait quietly for his demise, knowing it to be only a matter of time. An economic downturn could exacerbate this downfall just as it led to the government's defeat in 2002, which ushered in the Erdogan era. Continuing to force a more tyrannical government down everyone's throat is just as threatening to him, for another coup attempt is not out of the question.

In the meantime, the political instability in the Mid-East continues to grow, and a weak Turkey could contribute yet further to that instability. Of all Turkey's neighbors, Syria is in the most severe and present crisis in a region fraught with complex problems.

The Syrian Crisis

A peaceful uprising against the president of Syria almost nine years ago turned into a full-scale civil war. The conflict has left more than 360,000 people dead, devastated cities and drawn in other countries. Even before the conflict began, many Syrians were complaining about high unemployment, corruption and a lack of political freedom under President Bashar al-Assad, who succeeded his father, Hafez, after he died in 2000.

In of March 2011, pro-democracy demonstrations erupted in the southern city of Dara, inspired by the "Arab Spring" in neighboring countries. When the government used deadly force to crush the dissent, protests demanding the president's resignation erupted nationwide. The unrest spread and the crackdown intensified. Opposition supporters took up arms, first to defend themselves and later to rid their areas of security forces. Mr. Assad vowed to crush what he called "foreign-backed terrorism." The violence rapidly escalated and the country descended into civil war.

The Syrian Observatory for Human Rights, a UK-based monitoring group with a network of sources on the ground, had documented the deaths of 367,965 people by December 2018. The figure did not include 192,035 people who it said were missing and presumed dead. Meanwhile, the Violations Documentation Center, which relies on activists inside Syria, has recorded what it considers violations of international humanitarian law and human rights law, including attacks on civilians. It has documented 191,219 battle-related deaths, including 123,279 civilians, as of December 2018. (https://www.bbc.com/news/world-middle-east-35806229)

What is the war about?

It is now more than a battle between those who are for or against Assad. Many groups and countries – each with their own agendas – are involved, making the situation far more complex and prolonging the fighting. And this has also allowed the jihadist groups Islamic States (IS) and Al-Qaida to flourish. Syria's Kurds, who want the right of self-government but have not fought Mr. Assad's forces, have added another dimension to the conflict.

Who's involved?

The government's key supporters have been Russia and Iran, while Turkey, Western powers and several Gulf Arab states have backed the opposition.

Russia - which already had military bases in Syria - launched an air campaign in support of Mr. Assad in 2015 that has been crucial in turning the tide of the war in the government's favor. The Russian military says its strikes only target "terrorists" but activists say they regularly kill mainstream rebels and civilians.

Iran is believed to have deployed hundreds of troops and spent billions of dollars to help Mr. Assad. Thousands of Shia Muslim militiamen armed, trained and financed by Iran - mostly from **Lebanon's Hezbollah** movement, but also **Iraq, Afghanistan and Yemen** - have also fought alongside the Syrian army.

The **US, UK and France** initially provided support for what they considered "moderate" rebel groups. But they have prioritized non-lethal assistance since jihadists became the dominant force in the armed opposition.

A US-led global coalition has also carried out air strikes on IS militants in Syria since 2014 and helped an alliance of Kurdish and Arab militias called the **Syrian Democratic Forces (SDF)** capture territory once held by the jihadists in the east.

Turkey has long supported the rebels, but it has focused on using them to contain the Kurdish militia that dominates the SDF, accusing it of being an extension of a banned Kurdish rebel group in Turkey. Turkish-backed rebels have controlled territory along the border in north-western Syria since 2016.

Saudi Arabia, which is keen to counter Iranian influence, has armed and financed the rebels, as has the kingdom's Gulf rival, **Qatar.**

Israel, meanwhile, has been so concerned by what it calls Iran's "military entrenchment" in Syria and shipments of Iranian weapons to Hezbollah that it has conducted hundreds of air strikes in an attempt to thwart them. (https://www.bbc.com/news/world-middle-east-35806229)

Relations with Syria before the Civil War.

Turkey, under Erdogan and his foreign minister Ahmet Davutoglu, began a policy to seek warmer ties with its neighbors, including Syria, in the 2000s. Turkey very much wanted to have a greater influence over its much smaller neighbor to the south, especially relative to Iran. Erdogan courted the Assad regime at this point, with their families even vacationing together in 2008 (Cagaptay, 2017, p.163). Turkey lifted travel restrictions on Syrians and began more bilateral trade. But when open rebellion in Syria broke out in 2011, Erdogan could not convince Assad to implement reforms to quell the rebellion, nor stop brutalizing his own citizens. Erdogan found that the relationship they had built together could not stand the cold reality of civil war, and Assad's psychopathic drive to stay in power in his country at any cost, even that of killing tens of thousands of his own citizens.

This approach by Turkey demonstrated their history of seeking to find change within democratic means, which contrasted sharply with Assad's dictatorial and tyrannical madness. Eventually, Turkey broke off all diplomatic ties with Syria, putting it at odds with Iran, which, along with Russia, supported Assad in his slaughtering of his own citizens. Cagaptay (2017, p. 164) writes:

The reignited conflict with Tehran, Turkey's historical regional competitor, has led Ankara gradually to turn back towards the United States (in 2011 under Barack Obama) .... Washington and Ankara both hoped for a "soft landing" in Syria — not to mention an end to Assad's rule without the country descending into chaos.... Turkish cooperation with Washington in Libya — implemented after Ankara's initial reluctance to join military action against a Muslim leader — reinforced the United States positive view of Turkey.

This improved relationship with Turkey did not last long, unfortunately. This is because Turkey unilaterally decided to attempt a regime change in Syria, which the United States did not back. This unilateral action soured the relationship between them, which eventually led Turkey to reach out to China to purchase air defense systems that they would normally have purchased from the United States. Turkey hoped this would lead to a better deal with the U.S., but instead the move backfired and Turkey could not "plug-in" the newly purchased Chinese defense system into their existing NATO/U.S. defense systems. All of this further "soured" the relationship between Ankara and Washington. (Cagaptay, 2017, p. 166)

In the meantime the refugee crisis coming out of the war in Syria has been, and remains, immense. Beginning with a pre-wartime population of 22 million people, the United Nations (UN) has identified 13.5 million (2016) as requiring humanitarian assistance, of which more than 6 million (2016) are internally displaced, and around 5 million (2016) have now crossed national boundaries, with the majority being placed in Syrian refugee camps established in Turkey (3.6 million), Lebanon (1 million), Jordan (660 thousand), Egypt (130 thousand), and other countries since onset of the conflict in 2011. The Regional Refugee and Resilience Plan (3RP) was established in 2015, which is a coordination platform including neighboring countries—with the exception of Israel and Egypt. (https://data2.unhcr.org/en/situations/syria)

The United Nations High Commissioner for Refugees (UNHCR) counted almost 1 million (August 2017) asylum applicants in Europe. Turkey is the largest host country of registered refugees, with over 3.6 million Syrian refugees. Humanitarian aid to internally displaced persons (IDPs) within Syria and Syrian refugees in neighboring countries is planned largely through the UNHCR. By 2016, various nations had made pledges to the UNHCR to permanently resettle 170,000 registered refugees. Fears of being inundated by Syrian refugees has greatly affected politics within the European Union, most notably in Germany, which has absorbed—or rather is trying to absorb—hundreds of thousands of Syrian refugees, which has now become a national crisis leading to the rise of ultra-nationalist populist parties.

In Hungary, as previously mentioned, Victor Orban has sensationalized the fear of refugees and set himself up as the great Christian protector of Europe against the Muslim "hoards," rushing into Europe from the Middle East. His voters at home have largely bought this narrative, despite the fact that less than 1,000 refugees from Syria have actually been accepted by Hungary and that future plans are not to accept any. Orban has also used the opportunity to clamp down on democratic institutions within his country under cover of "protecting" his citizens. Other populist leaders in France, Poland, and the Czech Republic are now singing Orban's song within their countries, with Orban leading the chorus across Europe.

Not to be forgotten in this discussion is Putin's and Russia's role in supporting the Assad regime, which has led to the migrant crisis in Europe. The migrant crisis serves to destabilize the democratically elected governments in all of these countries, by providing fuel to bait voters with nationalist and populist rhetoric as a ruse while they quietly dismantle the democratic institutions within those countries. This is all part of Putin's disruptive global strategy as "Fire-Sower in-Chief".

That is not to say that strong immigration policies and borders don't have to be enacted. They most definitely do. But not as a "bait and switch" exercise where you awaken one day, in Hungary, for example, and find out that over the course of the government "protecting its citizens," the executive branch of government (i.e., the president) now controls all three branches of government (judicial, legislative, and executive), and further that the media has been silenced through government takeovers of news outlets, and "enemies" of the now one-party system, former legitimate opposition party members, are being jailed and/or killed.

More recently, in October of 2019, Erdogan convinced Donald Trump to withdraw American troops from northern Syria, thus enabling Turkey to rid itself of the opposition Kurds on their border (the formerly mentioned SDF), while creating a twenty mile "safe zone" on their southern border with Syria. This troubling move by Trump at once betrayed a long-time ally in the region, as the Kurds had lost 11,000 fighters defending the region with the United States. In one fell swoop, this manipulation of Trump by Erdogan a) exposed the Kurdish population to genocide by Turkish and other anti-Kurdish forces, b) left a power vacuum in the region which is now being filled by Syria, Iran and Russia and c) has re-invigorated ISIL in the region, whose tens of thousands of soldiers simply blended back in with the resident populations of the region, but who are now re-surfacing as the Americans pull out.

Historically, there are few other international blunders to compare with the magnitude of ignorance displayed by Trump here, who has made the United States much less safe as a result of being "played like a cheap fiddle" by Erdogan. The ramifications of this grand mistake by the Trump presidency will echo through the ages to come.

SUMMARY

All former great empires want to restore their greatness, and Turkey is no exception. The Ottoman Empire ruled wide swaths of Eastern Europe, Eastern Asia, the Middle East, and North Africa over an impressive 600 years of history. And so "'why can we not be great again?" say its leaders and citizens. For Mustafa Kemal Ataturk, in the 1920s and 1930s, after the First Word War and the dismantling of the Ottoman Empire, greatness came in the form of a secular society that was liberal and democratic and leaned heavily towards Europe and its values. For Recep Tayyip Erdogan, greatness is being redefined as taking the form of a Muslim-leaning theocracy that is becoming increasingly more autocratic and illiberal, ruled by a majority that does not respect the needs of its minorities, which make up half of the Turkish population. The failed coup attempt in 2016 has only emboldened Erdogan to dramatically crack down on his opposition and curtail further any true democratic reforms, capitalizing on the joint trauma of the national psyche. Along the way, he has alienated Turkey from several key players in the region, including Russia and Iran, as well as the United States, their greatest former ally and supporter. All of this while Erdogan pursues even greater illiberal policies, in an attempt to seize even greater power for himself. All the evidence to date points to Erdogan becoming even more of a tyrant.

Because of this virtual takeover by Erdogan, Turkey, which is a medium-sized power as a country today, may never fulfill its potential to become a major power. To do that, it would have to be a healthy democracy—a democracy in which all of its citizens' rights are taken into account, not just the one half of the population that Erdogan represents.

As things stand today, Erdogan, by alienating almost half the population, is ensuring they will not participate in building the nation to its full potential. And the potential instead is that many of these bright and educated minds will seek to live elsewhere in healthier democracies outside of Turkey, thus draining the country of its human capital. From this sublimatio perspective, 30,000 feet above the ground, it is not difficult to see that on this trajectory, Turkey will likely not become great again anytime soon. Meanwhile, the potential for disaster looms in the background.

CHAPTER NINE

Ukraine: The Alchemical Cauldron

What will become of civilization, and of man himself, if the hydrogen bombs begin to go off, or if the spiritual and moral darkness of State absolutism should spread over Europe.... The mass crushes out the insight and reflection that are still possible with the individual, and this necessarily leads to doctrinaire and authoritarian tyranny if ever the constitutional State should succumb to a fit of weakness.

— C.G. JUNG (1957, PP. 12–13)

In order to understand what is transpiring in the Ukraine presently, we must first understand the psychological dynamics of the two political philosophies that are at war there. These dynamics are explained astutely by the Yale historian Timothy Snyder in his recent book The Road to Unfreedom (2018, pp. 15–16). The Ukraine people were seeking freedom from Russia and what Snyder describes as their politics of eternity and turning towards a deeper association with the West and their politics of inevitability.

Snyder describes the politics of inevitability as that set of conservative beliefs in the West (America and Western Europe) that the capitalistic system works best when we allow the free market system to determine wealth and privilege with an absolute minimum of laws and regulations implemented by government. Further, this politics of inevitability is a never-changing perspective and should be treated as the undeniable truth of the matter always and at all times. There are no other ideas than this worthy of consideration in the running of a country or federation.

The politics of eternity is the system of government set up now in Russia, where there is no new history (so once again there are no new ideas), just the past forever repeating itself. For example, Russia is always at war with the evil West, and so must always be protecting and defending itself from its attacks. Because Russia was being attacked from the West, it had to invade Ukraine in 2014 in order to protect and defend itself. Russia and its citizens are innocents, and had no choice but to take action to protect "greater Russia," of which the Ukraine is considered part. Because Russia is constantly being attacked by the West, there is a demand to have a strong and centralized government (with a strongman as its leader) that is free of true elections that would only disrupt its smooth and consistent governing. Thus, succession in government (the democratic process of electing new governments every four or six years) becomes a thing of the past, as indeed it has become in Russia since its bogus elections of 2011.

Snyder (2018) argues that Russia reached the politics of eternity first, having established an oligarchy that was beholding to Putin and buttressed by the political philosophy of Ivan Ilyin, an early 20th-century Russian fascist. This philosophy has greatly helped Putin in his transitioning of Russia from a failed democracy to a successful fascist state in the 2010s. Snyder (2018) states:

> *The capitalist version of the politics of inevitability, the market as substitute for policy, generates economic inequality that undermines belief in progress. As social mobility halts, inevitability gives way to eternity, and democracy gives way to oligarchy. An oligarch spinning a tale of an innocent past, perhaps with the help of fascist ideas, offers fake protection to people with real pain. Faith that technology serves freedom opens the way to his spectacle. As distraction replaces concentration, the future dissolves in the frustrations of the present, and eternity becomes daily life. The oligarch crosses into real politics from a*

world of fiction, and governs by invoking myth and manu-
facturing crises. In the 2010s one such person, Vladimir
Putin, escorted another, Donald Trump, from fiction to
power. (pp. 15–16)

I find Snyder's concepts of the politics of inevitability and the politics of eternity to be useful ones as they lead us underneath to the psychology of what is at work in individuals who support these seemingly contradictory political philosophies. Of course there is a third option here, which Snyder eventually touches on, which would be a capitalistic system that is guided by the government and not allowed to function unconsciously on its own — a governing that consciously does its best to "level the playing field" between rich and poor, minorities and Whites, and helps to create and support a viable and substantial middle class for the majority of its citizens.

Thus, the frustrations of an unrestricted capitalistic system— the politics of inevitability — could not then be turned into a politics of eternity so easily, with a strong man seizing political power to supposedly "protect citizens" from the enemy outside its walls. Meanwhile, in fact, their leader along with his oligarchic cronies are stealing unabashedly from the State they have sworn to protect.

Both the politics of inevitability and the politics of eternity are spiritually vacuous, which tells us once again that the real problem is actually a spiritual one and that the politics presently manifesting are but a major symptom of the spiritual malaise that has infected both the East and the West. In any case our defenses against a global neo-fascist epidemic are currently in very bad shape.

Snyder (2018) goes on to outline the three main features of 1920s and 1930s European fascism:

1. It celebrated will and violence over reason; 2. It proposes
a leader with a mystical connection; and 3. It characterized

> *globalization as a conspiracy as opposed to a set of prob-*
> *lems. Revived today in conditions of inequality as a politics*
> *of eternity, fascism serves oligarchs as a catalyst for tran-*
> *sitions away from public discussion and towards political*
> *fiction; away from meaningful voting and towards fake*
> *democracy; away from the rule of law and towards person-*
> *alist regimes. (p.16)*

Ultimately, the politics of eternity is another philosophy that states that there are no ideas, only a repetition of the past in an eternal cycle. And given the huge disparity in wealth now in the United States, between the rich and the poor, it is easy to see how close we are to this reality. Wealthy ultra-right-wing industrialists in the United States, like the Koch brothers and their dark network of money, think tanks, and ultra-conservative nonprofits, are probably the best example of this. They use their wealthy influence to buy Republicans in the congress and senate, thus ensuring that their chosen policies, and not those of the American majority of people, are served.

One could also point to the power mongers who run the American health insurance and pharmaceutical industries, and suck billions of dollars of wealth out of the middle and lower classes every year in excessive profits, while illegally denying coverage at every opportunity. One can also add big oil, gas, and coal magnates to this list of entities that benefit from corporate welfare in the billions of dollars while killing the planet on which we live. (Maddow, 2019)

These American oligarchs are already living in their own version of the politics of eternity, which they consciously push for at every bought opportunity. They and others in the U.S. among the ultra-conservative one percent of the wealthy want and are getting the politics of eternity they have sought for decades now, and having an authoritarian fascist like Donald Trump in the oval office—delivered with an assist from Vladimir Putin, the oligarch-in-chief of Russia —is a dream come true.

Returning to the Ukraine, there is a background of warring political philosophies between the politics of inevitability in the West and a politics of eternity in Russia and the East. Both are fantasy worlds that do not take facts into account—the politics of inevitability because it lazily and unconsciously trusts that the capitalistic free market system will lead to equality and democracy on its own.

The politics of eternity is even more egregious, in that it consciously denies the facts of history. Snyder (2018) states: "The Russian politics of eternity reached back a thousand years to find a mystical moment of innocence. Vladimir Putin claimed (in 2011) that his millennial vision of the baptism of Volodymyr of Kyiv in the year 988 ce made Russia and Ukraine a single people" (p.111). This, despite the reality that Kiev had existed for about 800 years without any political connection to Russia at all. It was just another convenient made-up "fact".

This "fact" that was reasserted by Putin again in 2013, two months before Ukraine was to sign an Association Agreement with the European Union as a first step in hopefully becoming a full-fledged EU member state. Ukraine was taking this step as it saw it as the only way to curb an oligarchic system that was fully backed by Putin and Russia. As Snyder (2018) states: "Russia would attempt to halt this process on the grounds that nothing new can happen within its spiritual sphere of influence — the Russian world." (p. 112) His attempt to apply a Russian politics of eternity beyond Russia's borders had unintended consequences. Ukrainians responded by creating new kinds of politics. In other words, Ukrainians weren't buying the myth that Putin was trying to sell them. As Snyder points out (pp. 124–125) the reality is that Putin likely knew he could not sell Ukrainians on this idea, but that he wanted to at least sell it to the Russians at home, where they were already encased in the politics of eternity, beginning with his second illegal term in office that began with the fake elections of 2011, the date when the Russian democracy formally ended.

The Ukraine, during the 20th century, was twice absorbed by

empires, the Soviet Union and then Nazi Germany. Both were unsuccessful ultimately. But the question remains, "After empire, what is the next transition to?" Snyder argues that nation states are usually not attainable, and if they are, they are not sustainable because of the reality of empire building by stronger nations around them—which is an argument to integrate within a larger union, such as the European Union, for the sake of the nation's survival and well-being. Nation states before the First and Second World Wars were often more myths than reality, according to Snyder (2018, p. 120), as they were, in reality, a part of an empire rather than separate nation states. The United Kingdom and the Austro-Hungarian empires are two good examples of this point.

> With the breakup of the Soviet Union in the early 1990s, Ukraine was marked by takeovers in Soviet assets and clever arbitrage schemes. Unlike in Russia, in Ukraine the new class of oligarchs formed themselves into durable clans, none of which dominated the state for more than a few years at a time. And unlike Russia, in Ukraine power changed hands through democratic elections... Unlike in Russia, in Ukraine the European Union was seen as a cure for the corruption that hindered social advancement and a more equitable distribution of wealth. (Snyder, 2018, p. 122)

The association agreement with the European Union therefore was a crucial step that the then leader of the Ukraine, Viktor Yanukovych, had promised to sign. But after being influenced by Putin, in November of 2013, Yanukovych refused to sign the agreement with the EU. This was unacceptable to the Ukrainian people. They did not want a Russian-exported politics of eternity that allowed for no real democracy, and no succession of power from one government to the next. Nor did they wish to have a Russian-style kleptocracy. It was all of these things that they specifically did not want. Snyder (2018) then explains what happened next:

It is the investigative journalists who bring oligarchy and inequality into view. As chroniclers of the contemporary, they react first to the politics of eternity. In the oligarchical Ukraine of the twenty-first century, reporters gave their fellow citizens a chance at self-defense. Mustafa Nayyem was one of those investigative journalists and on November 21st, he had had enough. Writing on his Facebook page, Nayyem urged his friends to go out and protest. "Likes don't count," he wrote. People would have to take their bodies to the streets. They came to the Maidan square, in Kiev, and they stayed. And in so doing they took part in the creation of a new thing: a nation. In the beginning, students and young people, thousands of them from Kiev and around the country, came and stayed; the citizens with the most to lose from a frozen future. The violent crackdown by police was unexpected, given that Ukrainians had become accustomed for a generation to having the right of peaceful protest. (p.124)

But this crackdown only made things much worse for the authorities, as the students and journalists who had begun the protests were now joined by tens of thousands of others from every walk of life and social stratum, from the cities and the countryside; farmers, truckers, plumbers, teachers, academics, and homemakers swelled the ranks of the protests, which lasted for weeks in what became known as the Independence Square in Kyiv, the Maidan. Snyder (2018, p. 125) surmises: "The reflex of protecting the future, triggered in the minds of the students by the fear of losing Europe, was triggered in others by the fear of losing the one generation raised in an independent Ukraine."

Sadly, the West only took notice when there was bloodshed on the streets, and Russia used this as an excuse to invade the country and shed more blood. Top Russian leaders felt that invasion was necessary because if they didn't stand up to this nation building in Ukraine, the Russian people might get the idea that they could bring about the same changes in Moscow; and it is this idea that continues to terrify Putin and his oligarchs more than any other.

In January of 2014, the Yunakovych government passed a number of Russian-dictated laws to violently clamp down on the protests in the Maidan and make Yanukovych a puppet of Putin. These only backfired, however, as Ukrainians accurately saw these laws as an unwanted foreign intervention. Snyder (2018) notes the consequences of two protesters being shot on January 22:

> *The Maidan grew as never before. Remote-controlled counter-revolution had failed. Russia was unable to move Ukraine into Euroasia by helping Yanukovych to repress the opposition. It was time for a shift in strategy. By early February 2014, it appeared Moscow no longer aimed to maneuver Yanukovych and Ukraine into Eurasia. Instead, Yanukovych would be sacrificed to a campaign to provoke chaos throughout the country. (p. 135)*

This new shift in the dynamic was based on the assumption that if Russia invaded a part of the Ukraine, the provisional government would promptly fall apart. This belief was bolstered by fictitious reports on the internet that defined opponents of the Russians as being fascists and described Ukrainian atrocities being perpetrated in the Crimea. All of this fake news came compliments of Russian trolls let loose on the internet by the Internet Research Agency (IRG), a Russian government sponsored news agency based in St. Petersburg that later significantly influenced the 2016 Brexit vote in the United Kingdom and the 2016 American elections on behalf of Donald Trump. In Ukraine, this was the combination of a real war with a cyber-war, a now familiar tactic in Putin's playbook.

Despite all of these Russian efforts, the Ukrainian people were not playing by either the rules of the politics of eternity or the politics of inevitability. Instead they were creating a third option —which would occur through what Jung referred to as the transcendent function, which could create a new third thing out of the opposition of two perspectives. And the creative push came directly out of their own deeply held individual beliefs that they wanted a history of their own going forward. They did not want the politics of eternity that Putin was trying to sell them; and neither did they want a politics of inevitability whereby only the one percent are well served. And they now understood, in a very visceral way, that they had to be intimately involved in order for this to happen; they had to decide to risk their lives and go out into the cold winter streets and march for their freedom. No state or strongman was going to accomplish this for them. They realized in that moment that "we the people are the state." Snyder (2018) writes:

> *Beginning in February, 2014, some ten thousand Russian special forces, in uniform but without insignia, moved northward through the Crimean Peninsula. The moment they left their bases they were engaged in an illegal invasion of Ukraine. Kiev was caught by surprise at a moment when chains of command were uncertain and the main concern was to avoid further violence. Provisional Ukrainian authorities ordered Ukrainian forces on the peninsula not to resist. By the night of February 26, Russian soldiers had seized the regional parliament building in the city of Simferopol and raised the Russian flag...Having invaded Ukraine, Russian leaders took the position that their neighbor was not a sovereign state. This was the language of empire. (pp. 139-140)*

The head-spinning logic that the Ukraine was no longer a state because of the chaos caused by Russia invading it is a trademark of the Russian politics of eternity, and can only be considered for what it is; namely, predatory and delusional. But the spin doesn't stop there, as Russia then stated that the choice now in the Ukraine was between Russia and Nazism. If you accept that this is the actual choice, as either a Russian or Ukrainian citizen, then you have already colluded with the tyranny of the real fascists in this situation; the Russians and their illegal invasion of the Crimea. Russians predominantly went along with this belief, whereas Ukrainians did not. "On the ballot were two options, both of which affirmed the annexation of Crimea by Russia. The first option was to vote for the annexation of Crimea by Russia. The second was to restore the autonomy of the Crimean authorities, who had just been installed by Russia and requested annexation by Russia" (Snyder, 2018, p. 141).

In April of that year, Putin affirmed that the disintegration of the Ukrainian state was brought about "in the interests of Russia," followed by cyber-attacks on scores of Ukrainian companies and institutions. Meanwhile a Russian neo-Nazi named Pavel Gubarev proclaimed himself "people's governor" on May 1, on the logic that "Ukraine never existed." (as cited in Snyder, 2018, pp. 144–145)

Schizofascism: The New Fascism of Russian

This new Orwellian type of fascism now being practiced in Russia aims at calling all of their opponents fascists, whether they be Americans, Ukrainians, Israelis, or Jews of any nation. It is predicated on an understanding of the conflicts of World War II in which the fascism of Germany was defeated. The argument goes that fascism is an outgrowth of capitalism—and that German fascism is just one example of this. It assumes that further assaults from Western fascists everywhere are a constant threat that must be defended against by the innocent Russian state.

The toxic elements of the alchemy of tyranny are clear to see today, in both the Ukraine and in the United States. These elements consist of the underlying psychological warfare between the politics of eternity in the East and the politics of inevitability in the West. Both of these political philosophies are delusional in that they do not affirm the facts of history or that there can be anything "new" that is ever created politically. But that is their big lie, and to accept the lie is to give up our freedom. The reality is that it is imperative in this moment in history to look for new ideas and to understand that, psychologically speaking, we always have the ability to create a new and better reality if we have the individual and collective will to do so.

The old ruling principles of both the East and the West must now undergo a mortificatio, a death. And something new must take their place: namely, a better form of a truer democracy where there is a level playing field for all, where everyone is treated as an equal, and where the capital markets are guided by sound policies that benefit the greater good. These beneficent principles are within our collective grasp, if we have the consciousness and persistence to pursue them.

The association agreement between Ukraine and Europe was signed in June of 2014 and went into force in September of 2017. It is not solving all the problems inherent in running a new democracy. But the overall outcome is clear. The marching on the Maidan led by young people made a difference, and history is moving on. Something new, between the politics of inevitability and the politics of eternity, was born — has been newly created.

But first the Ukrainian people had to stand up for themselves against the tyranny of the Russian Federation. They had to put their own lives on the line to secure their own political freedom and control their own political future. No less will be required going forward in the rest of Europe and in the United States. And that time for us in America may be much nearer than we realize.

More recently, in September of 2019, it came to light, through a U. S. government whistleblower, that Donald Trump had asked the new president of the Ukraine, Vladimir Zelensky, to investigate Joe Biden and his son in exchange for providing the Ukraine with American military aid (for missiles) to defend against their Russian invaders. This "quid pro quo" is illegal to request of a foreign country and, more importantly, undermines the foreign policy of the United Sates in order for a personal favor to be granted to the president; namely investigating one of his main opponents in the 2020 election, Joe Biden.

A full impeachment enquiry into the matter has now been voted on by the Democratic-controlled House of Representatives, and the depth of this investigation has already revealed a wide-spread campaign by Trump and his associates to undermine our 2020 presidential election, dating back several months. On November 18, 2019 Donald J. Trump, the 45th president of the United States, was impeached by the democratically led House of Representatives for abuse of his power and obstruction of justice. The Republican–controlled senate has recently acquitted Trump of these charges, protecting him when they knew better. This has only emboldened Trump further, as he now feels he is totally above the law. The acquittal by the senate was, de facto, a coronation of Trump. The demolition of our democracy continues in real time.

CHAPTER TEN

Strange Magic: Understanding the Psychopathology of Tyrants

In actual fact, society is nothing more than an abstract idea like the State. Both are hypostatized, that is, have become autonomous. The State in particular is turned into a quasi-animate personality from whom everything is expected. In reality it is only a camouflage for those individuals who know how to manipulate it. Thus the constitutional State drifts into a situation of a primitive form of society, namely the communism of a primitive tribe where everybody is subject to the autocratic rule of a chief or an oligarchy.

— C. G. JUNG (1958, PP. 26–27)

Overview
The psychology of tyrants follows a very specific path that, although not surprising perhaps, demands elucidation. The one common thread of all tyrants is their narcissism. According to the Diagnostic and Statistical Manual of Mental Disorders — Fifth Edition (DSM-5, 2013, pp. 669–670, emphasis added),

> *The essential feature of Narcissistic Personality Disorder is a pervasive pattern of grandiosity, need for admiration, and lack of empathy that begins in early adulthood and is present in a variety of contexts.*

Narcissists typically exaggerate their achievements, and are often surprised when others do not share in their view of themselves (Criterion # 1). They tend to be obsessed with fantasies about their outstanding success, intellectual ability, power, and beauty (Criterion # 2). They have a tendency to believe that they are quite special and unique and therefore can only be understood by others who are also special and unique (Criterion # 3). They expect excessive admiration from others and are often puzzled when they do not receive it (Criterion # 4). They have a very keen sense of entitlement, that is, they expect to be treated differently because they are, in their eyes, special and unique. And if these expectations are not met, they can become extremely angry and volatile, lashing out at others around them (Criterion # 5).

Narcissists have a tendency to manipulate those around them to support them in their fantasy of how special and unique they are. They cultivate relationships with others who will support them in their fantasies (Criterion # 6). They have a distinct lack of empathy for others. That is, they do not have the reflective ability to understand how they may be emotionally affecting others around them by their behavior. And if brought to their attention, they most often deny and/or repress any awareness (Criterion # 7). Narcissists are usually envious of others and typically believe that others are also envious of them (Criterion # 8). Lastly, it is not uncommon for narcissists to demonstrate arrogant and haughty attitudes towards others (Criterion # 9).

Associated Features and Disorders

Underlying the positive inflation of narcissism there inevitably is a very severe negative inflation or inferiority complex within these individuals. In other words, their self-esteem is very low, which is the reason they had to construct the defense mechanism of the narcissism/positive inflation to begin with. Another way to describe this narcissism/positive inflation is to say they have a "superiority complex." The superiority complex then is a compensation for their poor self-esteem and inferiority complex. The DSM-5 (p. 671) goes on to state:

Vulnerability in self-esteem makes individuals with Narcissistic Personality Disorder very sensitive to "injury" from criticism or defeat. Although they may not show it outwardly, criticism may haunt these individuals and may leave them feeling humiliated, degraded, hollow, and empty. They may react with disdain, rage, or defiant counterattack. Such experiences often lead to social withdrawal or an appearance of humility that may mask and protect the grandiosity. Interpersonal relations are typically impaired due to problems derived from entitlement, the need for admiration, and the relative disregard for the sensitivities of others.

Nancy McWilliams states in her 2017 book Psychoanalytic Diagnosis (p.185):

One subtle outcome of the perfectionism of narcissistic people is the avoidance of feelings and actions that express awareness of either personal fallibility or realistic dependence on others. In particular, remorse and gratitude are attitudes that narcissistic people tend to deny ... remorse about some personal error or injury includes an admission of defect, and gratitude for someone's help acknowledges one's need. Because narcissistic individuals try to build a sense of self on the illusion of not having failings and not being in need, they fear that the admission of guilt or dependency exposes something unacceptably shameful. Sincere apologies and heartfelt thanks, the behavioral expressions of remorse and gratitude, may thus be avoided or compromised in narcissistic people, to the great impoverishment of their relationship with others.

It is not difficult to see the personalities of Vladimir Putin of

Russia, Victor Orban of Hungary, and Donald Trump of the United States come into full view at this point. And to this list we could add Milos Zeman of the Czech Republic, Recip Tayyip Erdogan of Turkey, and Bashar al-Assad of Syria. One never observes them accepting responsibility for anything wrong that happens. They are the innocent "blameless ones." They may often view themselves as the victims in a situation, when it suits them to do so; but they are never the perpetrators, though they may have to act at times to "protect" themselves, as Putin was apparently protecting Russia from the West by invading the Ukraine in 2014.

All of them have very thin skins (i.e., they are overly sensitive) and classically react when they have been ridiculed and humiliated with disdain, rage, and/or defiant counterattack. Putin reacts like this in a quiet, more introverted way; for example, having the Russian Foreign Intelligence service (the SVR, formerly known as the KGB) poison old political rivals living abroad, then pretending he had nothing to do with it. Trump reacts in more of an extraverted way, tweeting unceasingly about whomever has just gotten under his skin, which is very easy to do. One just has to criticize him and the tweeting will commence —be it a democratic official of color, a rogue white Republican who has the gumption to stand up to him, or immigrant Gold Star parents from the Middle East who don't agree with his policies. The DSM-5 (p. 671) goes on to state:

> *Sustained feelings of shame or humiliation and the attendant self-criticism may be associated with social withdrawal, depressed mood, and Dysthymic or Major Depressive Disorder. In contrast, sustained periods of grandiosity may be associated with a hypomanic mood. Narcissistic Personality Disorder is also associated with Anorexia Nervosa and substance-Related Disorders (especially related to cocaine). Histrionic, Borderline, Anti-social, and Paranoid Personality Disorders may be associated with Narcissistic Personality Disorder.*

To summarize, although Narcissistic Personality Disorder and its attendant symptoms may be the foundation of personalities like Putin, Orban, and Trump, this does not necessarily explain all of their bad behavior. For this reason, it is helpful to look to other psychological explanations beyond the DSM-5.

A Mythic Interlude

The classic version of the myth of Narcissus is by Ovid. While walking in the woods one day, Echo, a mountain nymph, sees Narcissus and falls in love with him. Narcissus senses he is being followed and shouts out, "who is there?" Echo repeated "who is there?" She later revealed herself to him, but he shunned her and told her to leave him alone. Nemesis, the goddess of revenge, later lured Narcissus to a pool of water when he was out hunting one day. When he peered into the water he saw his own reflection and fell in love with it, as if it was someone else. He eventually realized that his love could not be reciprocated, and he melted away under the force of his own burning passion; eventually turning into a gold and white flower.

What is worth noting on a psychological level is that Narcissus is unconscious of his own reflection; which ties into the fact that narcissists are incapable of "reflecting upon themselves." This creates all sorts of problems relating appropriately to other people. Another way to put it is that they are dissociated from themselves, which precludes them from relating deeply or meaningfully with others.

Malignant Narcissism

You will not find the concept of malignant narcissism in the DSM-5. It is, however, a very practical and effective explanation by which to grasp a fuller picture of the personality of tyrants. It was a term first coined by Erich Fromm, a well-known social psychologist of his generation, in 1964. Fromm defined malignant narcissism as a severe mental sickness representing the quintessence of evil. He characterized the condition as "the most severe pathology and the root of the most vicious destructiveness and inhumanity"

> *A common feature of narcissism is the reoccurring need to always be the center of attention. Their low self-esteem demands reinforcements, validation, and admiration at all times. However, this isn't the case in malignant narcissism. Those with this personality type have completely assumed their role of superiority and magnificence, and they don't doubt it for a second. The only thing they look for is to position themselves in a high rank wherever they go. Fromm described them as follows: "They feel powerful due to those qualities that they believe were given to them at birth. I'm better than you, therefore I don't need to prove anything. I don't need to interact with anyone or make any effort either. I move further and further away from reality the more I maintain this image of greatness" (https://exploringyourmind.com/malignant-narcissism-according-to-erich-fromm/).*

The primary difference between narcissism and malignant narcissism is that malignant narcissism includes comorbid features of other personality disorders, and thus consists of a broader range of symptoms than narcissistic personality disorder (NPD) alone. In malignant narcissism, NPD is accompanied by additional symptoms of antisocial, paranoid, and sadistic personality disorders. Whereas individuals with NPD will deliberately damage other people in pursuit of their own selfish desires, they may regret doing so and in some circumstances will show remorse for doing so. Because the traits of antisocial personality disorder (ASPD) are present in malignant narcissism, the malignant narcissist suffers from a more pervasive lack of empathy than someone with NPD alone and will lack feelings of guilt or remorse for any damage he or she causes.

Since sadism is often considered a feature of malignant narcissism, an individual with the syndrome may not only lack feelings of guilt or remorse for hurting others, but may even derive pleasure from the gratuitous infliction of mental or physical pain on others. These traits were formerly codified in the DSM-III under sadistic personality disorder (SPD). (American Psychiatric Association, 1980)

The American psychologist Theodore Millon claimed there were four subtypes of sadism, which he termed enforcing sadism, explosive sadism, spineless sadism, and tyrannical sadism. Millon described a tyrannical sadist as one who relishes menacing and brutalizing others, forcing them to cower and submit; verbally cutting and scathing, accusatory and destructive; intentionally surly, abusive, inhumane, unmerciful (Millon, 2000).

It is fair to apply the word evil to behaviors that idealize destructive aspects of the Self, and the sado-populist and sado-fascist behaviors practiced by individuals like Putin, Orban, and Trump would fit into the above description as would a hand to a well-fitted glove. As Snyder points out (p. 272):

> To proclaim "America First" was to deny any need to fight fascism either at home or abroad. When American Nazis and white supremacists marched in Charlottesville in August 2017, Trump said that some of them were "very fine people." He defended the Confederate and Nazi cause of preserving monuments to the confederacy. Such monuments in the American South were raised in the 1920's and 1930's at a time when fascism in the United States was a real possibility; they memorialized the racial purification of Southern cities that was contemporary with the rise of fascism in Europe.... A politician like Trump uses false beliefs about past and present to justify fictional policies that reaffirm those false beliefs, making politics an eternal struggle against enemies.

Snyder goes on to point out that the American politics of eternity generates policies whose whole point is to inflict pain. This includes giving the top one percent of the population a huge tax break financed by the lower and middle classes, and weakening the Affordable Care Act (also known as Obama-care), kicking thirteen million more people off of affordable health care insurance. The principle here is that "I don't mind suffering and being in pain as long as the other guy is suffering worse than me. Just give me my emotional hit every day/week by attacking Muslim immigrants, Blacks, Hispanics, and liberals and I'm happy to accept my pain." Snyder (2018, p. 275) states:

> On one level, a poor person, unemployed worker, or opioid addict who votes away health care is just giving money to the rich that they do not need and perhaps will not even notice. On another level, such a voter is changing the currency of politics from achievement to suffering, from gain to pain, helping a leader of choice establish a regime of sado-populism. Such a voter can believe that he or she will hurt enemies even more. The politics of eternity converts pain to meaning, and then meaning back into more pain.

In this way, we can say that the United States under Trump is becoming more like Russia, not just politically, but psychologically. In strategic relativism, Russia hurt but aimed to make others hurt more—or at least to convince the Russian population that others were hurting more. Russian citizens took the pain of European and American sanctions after the Russian invasion of Ukraine in 2014 because they believed that Russia was in a glorious campaign against Europe and America and that Europeans and Americans were getting their just deserts for their decadence and aggression. A fictional justification for war creates real pain that justifies the continuation of a real war. In winning a battle of that war, in helping Trump to become president, Moscow was spreading this very logic inside the United States (Snyder, 2018, p. 275). This is the situation as Jung (1957, p. 13) may have seen it when he stated:

Rational argument can be conducted with some prospect of success only so long as the emotionality of a certain situation does not exceed a certain critical degree. If the affective temperature rises above this level, the possibility of reason's having any effect ceases and its place is taken by slogans and fantasies. That is to say a sort of collective possession results which rapidly develops into a psychic epidemic.

Trauma, Time, Truth and Trump

In her article *Trauma, Time, Truth and Trump: How a President Freezes Healing and Promotes Crises*, (2017) Betty Teng makes the point that in the days following the election of Donald Trump, many people in the United States felt traumatized, particularly those groups that were personally attacked by him during the election campaign, including Mexicans, African Americans, immigrants of color, and women. The level of disbelief that this reality television guy Trump could actually get elected to the highest office in the land seemed overwhelmingly surreal.

The American Psychological Association (2017) defines trauma as "an emotional response to a terrible event like an accident, rape, or natural disaster" (online). As Teng states (2017, p. 221)

And for many people — especially, but not confined to, those groups that Trump targeted during his campaign — his election and now his presidency are truly terrible, even disastrous events.... Indeed, in the months since November (2016) psychotherapists nationwide have reported an unprecedented focus on politics in their sessions, and a surge of new patients (Gold 2017) seeking help with the high anxiety and stress they feel in reaction to Trump's steady stream of extreme tweets and impulsive actions.... Trump appears to be more concerned with drawing attention to his power through creating crises rather than resolving them.

This surge of a free-floating anxiety due to Trump being in office is a fact I can attest to in my own analytic practice in Los Angeles over the past three years. And the anxiety and concern has not abated. It may even have become worse over that time period. "PTSD-like symptoms of insomnia, lack of focus, hyper-vigilance, irritability, and volatility now afflict not only combat veterans, first responders, and survivors of rape, violent crime, natural disaster, torture, and abuse, but many of the rest of us as well." (Teng, 2017, p. 221)

Our ability to understand trauma is contingent upon time. We can only appreciate what has happened in the past tense. And to do this requires time and a safe place in which to reflect upon this reality. This is what often can be achieved in therapy over a period of time and through much reflective effort to work down and through difficult traumatic events in a person's life. But in the Twitter-happy world of Trump, there is no reflective time provided in which healing can take place; only opportunity for more exhaustive tweeting to occur, and that is therefore a very unhealthy environment for all of us. The malignant narcissist Donald J. Trump has created an alternate form of reality in which he and his followers live; and as a result, we all get dragged along in the undertow of that fantasy world with all its strange magical thinking.

Impeachment

In February of 2020, Trump was acquitted from impeachment by the Republican led Senate. Upon his acquittal, Trump did not demonstrate any remorse or guilt for his illegal actions in attempting to bribe a foreign nation to help him cheat to get re-elected in a domestic election. He maintained that "it was a perfect call!" to the Ukrainian president, who was being requested to directly interfere in the American election by Trump.

This behavior is entirely consistent with that of a malignant narcissist. Instead, Trump felt emboldened to go on a revenge tour persecuting his "enemies" who were not loyal to him throughout the impeachment crises. That these individuals were loyal to the constitution of the United States does not count a wit for Trump. It is only loyalty to him that counts. This is how a dictator behaves in a third world country, or a mafia boss in New York City. This is our current president. It appeared that our newly crowned American emperor could never be either indicted or impeached; that he is above the law. But then something unforeseen by Trump (though not by others) happened in a "wet market" in Wuhan, China; and a world-wide corona virus pandemic was born.

The Trauma of the Covid – 19 Pandemic

As the apex of the Covid – 19 pandemic sweeps across the United States, we are again reminded daily of the malignant narcissism of our president. In his daily White House briefings, Trump goes out of his way to contradict his medical advisors, plant false stories along with false hope, and personally attack any journalist who asks a question he doesn't like. His embarrassment to the United States, both internally and externally, has only been accentuated. Deservedly, his approval numbers have plummeted.

His carnival barking about the corona virus cannot detract the rest of us away from the seriousness of the epidemic we are all facing together. Fortunately, strong leadership from national medical experts and state governors, along with scores of local officials, are leading most of us in the right direction, even as Trump repeatedly stumbles and obfuscates.

On a more positive note, his behavior also demonstrates the fact that, unlike Putin in Russia or Orban in Hungary, Trump is simply too lazy to seize control of the country in a more autocratic way, using the pandemic crises as an excuse. Windsor Mann, in a brilliant essay in the Los Angeles Times (Sunday, April

12, 2020) stated:

> *Trump prefers fake problems to real problems because real problems demand real solutions, which demand real work. Trump doesn't like to work and rarely does...He spends most of his time watching TV, tweeting and talking on the phone...In addition to being too lazy to do things, Trump is uninterested in doing things. He's interested in having things. This is what makes his narcissism malignant rather than benign. As the social psychologist Erich Fromm observed, narcissists derive their self-worth from their possessions, not from achievements...Subverting democracy requires more effort than Trump is willing to exert. He wants to be a dictator, but he's unwilling to do the work to become one. Just as he inherited a fortune, he wants to inherit an autocracy. To be a strongman, you have to have a strong work ethic. Trump has only weak ethics.*

Trump has "led from behind" throughout the pandemic, at first downplaying its importance and then describing it simply as a democratic "hoax." Thousands of Americans are now dying from the pandemic. Clearly many less deaths would be occurring if Trump had chosen to not be so bombastic and lethargic in response to it. Instead, in the typical fashion of the malignant narcissist he is, he seeks to blame others for any problems while maintaining that he did everything right. Esther Harding (1947), in relation to this, stated:

> *Just as a negative inflation brings life to a standstill, so a positive inflation, causing the ego to feel itself powerful, dominant and "always right," is likewise against life. For a person whose ego suffers from such an invasion of non-personal powers does not contact life directly either. Instead of facing life and its tasks realistically on the level of ac-*

tual attainments, he approaches them with the assumption that he is master. He identifies himself unconsciously with some great figure, Napoleon or Beethoven or Christ. Such an image is technically called the archetype of the "mana personality." Perhaps the man's assumption of superiority works; then those around him will pay him the deference his attitude demands and follow his leadership. If this happens, he may succeed, for as long as the identification continues to be effective. But he will remain undeveloped as a human being, as a man, for instead of living his own life, he is living the life of an archetypal figure endowed with non-personal powers. While the identification holds, he feels himself to be in control; actually, however, his psyche has been invaded and he himself has very little to say about his own acts and thoughts. If identification with the powerful archetype becomes complete, he will have lost his humanity, that is to say, he will be insane. (Psychic Energy, 1947, p. 228-229)

Whether Trump is in the process of becoming insane, or has actually achieved that level of psychopathology is an open question. But the psychic virus that he has infected the United States and the rest of the world with is just as dangerous as the corona virus. And has been spreading for a longer period of time. Hopefully the vaccine for Trump will be found soon.

EPILOGUE

Freedom versus Tyranny

Whoever, by election or caprice, gets into one of these positions (of governing) is no longer subservient to authority, for he is the State policy itself and within the limits of the situation can proceed at his own discretion. With Louis the XIV he can say, "L'etat c'est moi." He is thus the only individual or, at any rate, one of the few individuals who could make use of their individuality if they only knew how to differentiate themselves from the State doctrine. They are more likely however to be slaves of their own fictions.... Furthermore, in order to compensate for its chaotic formlessness, a mass always produces a "Leader," who almost infallibly becomes the victim of his own inflated ego-consciousness, as numerous examples in history show.

— C.G. JUNG (1957, P. 23)

For all our darker impulses, for all our shortcomings, and for all of the dreams denied and deferred, the experiment begun so long ago, carried out so imperfectly, is worth the fight. There is, in fact, no struggle more important, and none nobler, than the one we rage in the service of those better angels who, however besieged, are always ready for battle.

— ABRAHAM LINCOLN (AS CITED IN MEACHAM, 2018, P. 272)

We stand now at a stunningly distinct crossroads in American and global history. The encroachment of tyranny and tyrannical rule in Europe, Asia, and

America is becoming a smothering daily reality. Democracy and democratic rights for all citizens are slipping away day after day, and for the moment at least, the tyrannical Trump, a pathological liar and malignant narcissist, is triumphing over the democratic beliefs of a majority of American citizens. Attacks on the free press, voting rights, the courts, intelligence agencies, Blacks, Hispanics, Muslims, Jews, and immigrants in general continue unabated.

It is no longer just a conspiracy theory to understand that white supremacists all over the world are hoping and readying for a global race war fanned by the flames of racist rhetoric by tyrannical leaders in countries such as the United States (Donald Trump), Great Britain (Boris Johnson), Russia (Vladimir Putin), Czech Republic (Milos Zeman), and Hungary (Victor Orban). Other illiberal democracies with non-white populations are now appearing in countries such as Turkey (Recep Tayyip Erdogan), India (Narendra Modi), and Brazil (Jair Bolsonaro). These sado-populist regimes are fixated on a projection of the shadow onto the "other." For they themselves are blameless, and all of the problems in their countries are clearly not within themselves or with their policies, but with those who are different from them.

For those of us who have attained a certain age, it seems quite surreal that we would be, in the 2020's, at the threshold of another fascist crisis a mere 75 years after World War II was fought and won against Hitler and the Nazis. And yet here we are. It reminds one of the quote attributed to Thomas Charlton in 1909 of the necessity of "fastening upon the minds of the American people the belief that the price of freedom is eternal vigilance," and the late President Harry Truman who stated, "The next generation never learns anything from the previous one until it's brought home with a hammer... I've wondered why the next generation can't profit from the generation before but they never do until they get knocked on the head by experience." (as cited in Meacham, 2018 p. 259)

The Alchemy of Freedom

The only antidote for the alchemy of tyranny is something stronger that can stand up to it—what I call the alchemy of freedom. Tyranny is made up of the toxic elements of inequality, divisiveness, repetitive lies and conspiracy theories, fear, hate, and anger. These are all unconscious shadow properties of the mob that has been infected with a lethal psychosis by malignant narcissistic leaders in their populations. These are largely people who believe their leaders have their best interests at heart and will protect them, when in reality they are being exploited by those leaders as mere objects. All of these unconscious shadow properties are then projected onto the other; the brown people, the black people, the Muslims, the Jews, the people who look different from "us decent white folks" and who threaten us daily and constantly. How exactly, one is not sure, but W. B. Dubois (1935) may have put it most succinctly when he stated:

> Back of the writhing, yelling, cruel-eyed demons who break, destroy, maim and lynch and burn at the stake, is a knot, large or small, of normal human beings, and these human beings at heart are desperately afraid of something. Of what? Of many things, but usually of losing their jobs, being declassed, degraded, or actually disgraced; of losing their hopes, savings, their plans for their children; of the actual pangs of hunger, of dirt, of crime. (as cited in Meacham, 2018, p. 4)

The alchemy of freedom consists of the elements of equality, individuality, integration, truth, and a true democracy with government succession. Specifically, freedom is based upon the ability to differentiate truth from fiction—and to be able to do this one must be able to reflect and think things through. One must not just accept anything one reads or sees on a video or podcast, no matter the source. One must think as an individual, not as part of a mob infected with a psychosis induced by a so-called leader of a country who happens to be a malignant narcissist. This requires discipline and effort of will. This demands paying attention. This demands an eternal vigilance. This is the price of freedom.

The psychological reality of the present time is that we are woefully unconscious, individually and collectively. This is true not only of Americans, but also of Europeans and Asians and people the world over. And as Jung has pointed out, it is only each individual, one person at a time, who can become more conscious. And the question he raised then is the same as today: Will there be enough conscious individuals in the world to prevent us from destroying ourselves? In 1957, just twelve years after World War II had been fought and won against fascism, Jung stated:

> *Happiness and contentment, equability of soul and meaningfulness of life—these can be experienced only by the individual and not by the state, which, on the one hand, is nothing but a convention of independent individuals and, at the other, continually threatens to paralyze and threaten the individual. The psychiatrist is the one who knows most about the condition of the soul's welfare, upon which so infinitely much depends in the social sum. The social and political circumstances of the time are certainly of considerable significance, but the importance for the weal or woe of the individual has been boundlessly overestimated in so far as they are taken for the sole deciding factors. In this respect our social goals commit the error of overlooking the psychology of the person for whom they are intended and— very often—of promoting only his illusions.... I am neither spurred on by excessive optimism nor in love with high ideals, but am merely concerned with the fate of the individual human being—that infinitesimal unit on whom a world depends, and in whom, if we are to read the Christian message aright, even God seeks his goal. (pp. 124–125)*

REFERENCES

Albright, Madeline (2018). Fascism: A Warning. Harper-Collins. New York.

American Psychological Association. (2017). Many Americans Stressed about Future of Our Nation, New APA Stress in American Survey Reveals. APA.org, February 15. www.apa.org/news/press/releases/2017/02/stressed-ntion.aspx.

Barnes, Julian E., and Cooper, Helen (2018). Trump Discussed Pulling U.S. From NATO, Aides Say Amid New Concerns Over Russia. New York Times, January 14th.

Edinger, Edward F. (1984). The Eternal Drama; The Inner Meaning of Greek Mythology. Boston & London, Shambhala,

Edinger, Edward F. (1985). Anatomy of the Psyche; Alchemical Symbolism in Psychotherapy. Open Court Press, La Salle, Illinois.

Fromm, Erich. (2019). (https://exploringyourmind.com/malignant-narcissism-according-to-erich-fromm/.

Grevatt. William K. (2018). Confronting the Trickster: Crises and Opportunity in the Time of Trump. A Jungian Perspective. Psychological Perspectives, 61 (1), 43-47.

Havel, Vaclav. (1994). Speech to the European Union in Strasburg, France. March 8th. http://www.europarl.europa.eu

Jung, C. G. (1954). On the Psychology of the Trickster Figure. Volume 9.1, The Archetypes of the Collective Unconscious., R.F.C. Hull, Trans., H. Read, M. Fordham, G. Adler, & W. McGuire, Eds. Bollingen Series XX. Princeton, NJ: Princeton University Press.

Jung, C. G. (1954). Psychology and Alchemy. Volume 12 of the Collected Works. R.F.C. Hull, Trans., H. Read, M. Fordham, G. Adler, & W. McGuire, Eds. Bollingen Series XX. Princeton, NJ: Princeton University Press.

Jung, C. G. (1957). The Undiscovered Self. Little, Brown & Company, New York.

King, Laura (2018). Getting Even Tougher Against Migrants. Los Angeles Times Article, June 29th. Pages A-1 and A-4.

Kirchick, James (2017). The End of Europe; Dictators, Demagogues, and the Coming Dark Age. Yale University Press. New Haven & London.

Lee, Bandy, editor (2017). The Dangerous Case of Donald Trump; 27 Psychiatrists and Mental Health Experts Assess a President. Thomas Dunne Books; St. Marten's Press; New York.

Meacham, John (2018). The Soul of America; The Battle for Our Better Angels. Random House, New York.

McWilliams, Nancy (2017). Psychoanalytic Diagnosis; Understanding Personality Structure in the Clinical Process; second edition. Guilford Press, New York.

Maddow, Rachel (2019). Blowout: Corrupted Democracy, Rogue State Russia, and the Richest, Most Destructive Industry on Earth. Crown, New York.

Meyer, Jane (2016). Dark Money; The Hidden History of the Billionaires Behind the Rise of the Radical Right. 2016. New York, Doubleday

Meyer, Jane (2018). New Evidence Emerges of Steve Bannon and Cambridge Analytica's

Role in Brexit. New Yorker Magazine, online, November 17th.

Millon, T. (2000). Personality disorders in modern life. Hoboken, NJ: Wiley.

Neumann, Erich (1954). The Origins and History of Consciousness. New York, Pantheon.

Revel, Jean Francois (1983). How Democracies Perish. Doubleday, New York.

Snyder, Timothy (2017). On Tyranny; Twenty Lessons from the Twentieth Century. Tim Duggan Books; New York.

Snyder, Timothy (2018). The Road to Unfreedom; Russia, Europe, America. Tim Duggan Books; New York.

Taker, Michael and Wines, Michael (2018). Trump Disbands Commission on Voter Fraud., New York Times, January 3rd.

Various Authors; (2013) Diagnostic and Statistical Manual of Mental Disorders – Fifth Edition; American Psychiatric Association. Washington, DC.

UNCHR (2019). Where Have All the Syrian Refugees Gone? https://data2.unhcr.org/en/situations/syria

Woodward, Bob, 2018. Fear; Trump in the Whitehouse. Simon & Schuster, New York.